Introduction

Prostate Cancer
-a race between two snails

Introduction

Copyright ©2019 David Meredith

David Meredith has asserted his right under the Copyright, Designs and Patents Act 1988 to be identified as the author of this work. All rights reserved.

No part of this publication may be reproduced, stored in a retrieval system or transmitted in any form, or by any means (electronic, mechanical or otherwise) without the prior written permission of the copyright owner.

Cover design: David Meredith

Drawings: David Meredith

Book title credit: John Cobb

This book is intended to be a light-hearted account of my Prostate Cancer experience, designed to provide a little guidance and support for anyone going through something similar. Nothing in the book should be relied on as medical or nutritional advice. If you have any medical conditions or doubt about your health you should contact a qualified medical professional.

To June Meredith
-who has suffered so much and for so long

Introduction

Prostate Cancer affects one man in eight in the UK. By the time its symptoms have become apparent it's often too late for it to be cured. The answer is to get yourself checked out.
I was lucky. I had a warning sign. Millions of others don't get one.

Introduction

Do you have a relative who has been diagnosed? Are you worried about Prostate Cancer? Do you want to know what the treatment involves? What it's **actually like** to go through it? Would you benefit from another person's first-hand experience?

There are many men, and I was one, who believe that ignorance is bliss. That Prostate Cancer can't happen to them and by ignoring the signs it will go away. There are others who stubbornly refuse to get tested and dismiss the risk with a resigned shrug. A fatalistic attitude that demands that they should simply accept their fate.

I've written this book to show people what is involved. That if I can confront it -you can too. When I was diagnosed, I was swamped with factual information, the reasons for the treatments and their side-effects, but precious little on what it would **feel** like to go through it. I wanted a book written by an ordinary person who was enjoying life, and someone who'd got through to the other side without having to be a super-hero. There's no resorting to private treatment here. No long lingering appointments with the surgeon. No time to get on first-name terms with the consultant while you discuss your pathology report. This book relates the glacially slow NHS journey that most of us will face, plus a few complications thrown in for dramatic effect.

This book is aimed at those who have just been diagnosed, their relatives, those who are curious, but principally those who are reluctant to seek help.

This is the story of my personal battle with prostate cancer. It's not a medical book as such, but there's enough medical information to satisfy the curiosity of most people. Beware though! It's intimate

Introduction

and candid and the reader is spared nothing. You'll probably find out more about the author than it would be wise to know about anybody! I hope you will find it a humorous, heart-warming and sympathetic account.

Follow me into the hospital and strap yourself in for the ultimate white-knuckle ride!

Introduction

CONTENTS

1. Investigations

2. Biopsy

3. The Catheter Years Part 1

4. Results

5. Waiting for the bone scan results

6. Discussing the options

7. The Catheter Years Part 2

8. The Operation

9. Recovery

10. All is revealed

11. What was it like for you darling?

12. Looking Forward

Postscript

Appendix

Investigations

1 Investigations

'Please try and stay calm Mr Meredith. Prostate Cancer is very slow moving'
'So's the bloody treatment' I thought to myself '-like a race between two snails'.
'Sorry to bother you Kate, but I know so little about it' I replied.
Kate was the nurse assigned to my case. She probably had a million other things to do. I really didn't want to bother her, but the weeks were passing by. I'd chosen to have my prostate removed but before they would even commit to doing it, I needed to have a bone scan. I already knew what this meant. My father had died of Prostate cancer after it had spread to his bones.
Diagnosed at 67. Dead at 69.
I'd just asked her if I could bring the scan forward by having it done privately, but she had assured me it wouldn't make any difference.
'I'll see if I can get it brought forward. Sometimes there are cancellations.'
I knew this was highly unlikely, but nevertheless I was re-assured.
'Ok thanks Kate. Sorry to bother you.'
'It's really no trouble Mr Meredith.'
I put the phone down.
You want them to say 'It will be fine'.
But they can't. They don't know. Nobody knows. Yet.

I'd phoned her from my place of work -SCB. A high-tech company making, - well actually I can't say. Not allowed to say.
But even if I told you, you'd die of boredom about two sentences in. We make products that save lives in far-away countries, and they are painted a sandy colour before leaving the premises. SCB -

Sandy Coloured Boxes. There you are. I've already said too much. I could be arrested before I get to the next page.

I looked at Kate's business card. Now hers really was a life and death job.

I stood up and walked to the conference room door. Provided it wasn't booked for a meeting, it was an ideal place for a private phone call. Before I opened it, I composed myself. Put my 'face' back on. Then I walked into a large open-plan office.

I needed to ask a favour of someone. I'd prepared for this by going to Greggs and buying some doughnuts before I came to work.

'Glenn?'

He looked up.

I took a step back: 'Christ, your good looking!'

'I think he wants something!' came a distant voice.

'Alright Dave, what do you want?'

'Is it possible to move this address line further over?'

He whistled between his teeth.

'For anybody else -yes. But for you?'

Some verbal sparring was always a necessary prerequisite in these situations.

'Be nice. There's a doughnut at stake!'

He laughed. I was half way there.

'Trouble is, we'll have to re-configure the wiring to the connector'.

I provided some technically sound reasons. I could still do it despite everything that was going on.

He gave a resigned shrug: 'Yeah ok then.'

I placed a bag on his desk and I was off.

'Thanks Glenn!'

'Ok Dave!'

A head popped up from a nearby desk:

'Check it Glenn. Make sure he hasn't licked all the sugar off!'

Investigations

I had cancer. Who knew?

My wife June and I were in the pub that evening with friends. Anne and John. Anne was June's bestie. She knew how to shop. June was an amateur by comparison. Stores took on extra staff when Anne was in town. She had some real purchasing power, but what the shops failed to realise was that most of it would be heading back their way, once she'd tried it on at home. We shared this standing joke where the girls were out shopping together. I would be monitoring our bank account on-line and watching the bank balance change like the numbers on a fruit machine. Of course, they never did.

Andrew was one of the kindest people I'd ever met. If you were going to a pub he'd always rush ahead and open the door for you - so you could get to the bar first. His carefulness was legendary. He could make a tea bag last all day. He would claim he was doing his bit for the planet. Most people would think he was just being tight.

We'd known them a long time. Nothing was off limits. I updated them on my phone call. They made supportive noises.

'I can't complain' I mused, '..I'm 62 years old and this will be my first time in hospital.'

'No it isn't! What about that time you went in for your vasectomy?' asked June, helpfully.

'Yes, but I didn't stay in overnight.'

'I didn't know you'd had the snip' said John.

I recalled my only previous brush with the medical profession:

'There were about half a dozen of us sat in our operation gowns, waiting nervously in an ante-room before being called in for the operation. A nurse tried to distract us by turning the television on.

It was racing from Doncaster. The 3.15pm race for geldings' I laughed.
There was a collective groan from around the table.
I could see John instinctively push his hands between his legs.
'I was just glad I had a general anaesthetic' I concluded.
Anne looked puzzled.
'I thought they were done under local anaesthetic?'
I couldn't help myself now, I was being presented with an open goal:
'They must have taken one look at it and realised that it would have to be a general!'
'Yeah right!' she laughed.
'It took two of them to bring it under control!' I protested.
Out of the corner of my eye I saw June raise her hand and hold her thumb and forefinger about an inch apart.
They were in gales of laughter.
Anne looked at me:
'What about Madeira?'
We'd shared a holiday with them a few years back.
'Yes!' June laughed 'His shorts came down in the sea!'
I had been the victim of a particularly large wave.
'That water was really cold!' I protested.
'We thought you'd had a sex change!' said John.
We were all laughing now. I was just an object of mirth. They were all getting in on the act:
'I remember Dave swimming like mad, and getting nowhere!'
'Yeah, in a foot of water!' laughed June.
'Well, I was probably dragging along the bottom!'
Anyway, dear reader. As I've said to people on many occasions:
'It's not how big your wand is – it's how much magic you've got in it!'

I had delusions of grandeur in the love-pump department, but it was no use making wild claims in front of Anne and John. They'd seen the reality. June sarcastically nicknamed me 'Big Dick' right from the start of our relationship. 'B.D.' for short. Sex should be fun -not something you prepared for by going to the gym. Especially once the serious business of having a family was out of the way. My advice to her if we were in that kind of mood consisted of two words: 'brace yourself!' So where does myth finish and reality start? We're twelve pages in dear reader and getting to know each other, so I'll share this with you. I'm small……..but quick.

It was the summer of 2016. I winced. I flushed the loo and washed my hands.
'You're going to have to go to the Doctor with that' said June.
Being a man meant your default response in this situation was to cross your fingers and hope it would go away. Doctors were for emergencies. I didn't even know the name of mine.
'I'll see if it's any better tomorrow.'
See what I mean? Typical.

'I think you have a UTI.'
The doctor caught my puzzled look.
'A urinary tract infection' she continued.
I guessed she was about mid-forties? She was business-like. We hadn't met before, but we skipped the formal introductions. I don't think she appreciated just how rare an occasion this was. An obscure name on the surgery database has just turned up like a long-lost person. Somebody must have gone off with a torch to find my medical records. I could imagine them heaving open the creaking door of a long-forgotten vault, and blowing the dust off

some a bit of parchment. I don't think she appreciated the fact she was more likely to see a solar eclipse.

'It's mainly women who get UTI's.' she said, looking at her screen.

'It's unusual for a man to get them because their urethras are longer,'

Then, turning towards me, she continued:

'..although UTI's are slightly more common in elderly gentlemen.'

Oooh! Nice. I shuddered.

The 'E' word. I let the word 'elderly' occupy my consciousness for several moments in an act of self-mutilation. I toyed with it. Tried it on for size. She had used the word without a moment's hesitation. I looked around. There was no one else in the surgery. It had to be me. She definitely used the word. It was like an arrow to the heart. I could still wipe my own bottom. My dentist advised me to floss my teeth to guard against gum disease. She clearly thought I had a future. When my doctor looked at me she saw ramps, grab-rails and wheelchairs. Assistance at airports. Food blenders. Maybe I should hand in my organ donor card. I still kept it on the basis that I accepted returns. She was still talking while I took stock of my new station in life. No wonder I never came here. She wrote out a prescription for some antibiotics and gave me a plastic jar for a urine sample.

'We may need to prescribe something different once we know exactly which virus we're dealing with'.

I was normally the most inquisitive person in the world, but with regard to medical matters, ignorance was bliss. It really was. Honestly -take it from me. I'm never ill.

'Tablets' I thought to myself. I counted my blessings. I could manage them. At least I didn't have to lie on the bed and be interfered with. I'd never had an internal examination. Didn't want to start now.

'I'm afraid I've got to ask a few personal questions regarding your sex life.'

Blimey, I was 60 years old. This wouldn't be a long discussion. I had never really been considered a sex object. 'Hard to believe' I hear you say, but it's true. I really wasn't that interesting.

'Okay..'

'Have you had more than one sexual partner recently?'

'No. I have a pretty uneventful life in that department.'

Despite my fantasies it was undeniably true. Women had always found me resistible. Even in my teens I'd been dimly aware of being left unattended by the opposite sex. The only person to ever give me a second glance was the undertaker.

She smiled. Didn't look entirely convinced. Not sure why. Anyway, I was happily married.

'Sorry. I had to ask. Don't forget the urine sample and be sure to take all the tablets.'

In my enlightened state nowadays, I realise that the reason you take all the tablets (even though you might be feeling better) is that the virus has to be completely wiped out. They are clever little buggers. If enough of them survive they can mutate and become immune to the antibiotic. Truly a nightmare scenario.

I played skittles for a team at my local pub. It was a game peculiarly popular in my part of the world. Despite my best efforts they'd finished top of the league. We'd been out on the town celebrating. I'd had a few to drink, and at the end of the night I got ready to cycle home. I un-padlocked my bike and switched my lights on. No

helmet though. I know. I know. I didn't need one. I was going to live forever.
Then I was on my way. Street lights passed overhead.

My eyelids opened. They were heavy. It was like raising an up-and-over garage door. I was sat on a cold hard pavement, my back to a wall. I tried to get up.
'No stay there' came a woman's voice 'You've been knocked off your bike.'
'Where is it?'
'It's ok. We're looking after it'.
I thought I could stand, but the effort was too much. I slumped back down.
I felt my eyes shutting. I should try and stay awake.
There was a face in front of them. A man's voice:
'You alright mate?'
My eyes may have re-opened but they weren't really helping. I couldn't make sense of my surroundings. Then there were flashing blue lights. Distorted radio communications.
I was led to an ambulance. A uniform asked me for my name and address. It required every bit of concentration I possessed to answer this fundamental question. I just wanted to go home – there was no need for all this fuss. I spoke to the medic in the ambulance. It was quite an effort to maintain a conversation but I persevered in an attempt to drive my recovery forwards. If I could convince the medic I was perfectly alright, they might just take me home. No questions asked. I'd be fine in the morning. Honest.
Unbeknown to me I had matted blood in my hair and a blood-stained face. I wasn't going to convince anyone that I was fit to go

home. I was disorientated. I was aching in lots of places and talking rubbish. Even more than usual. The medic knew I was. Everyone did. Except me.
I couldn't join things up. There had been a schism in reality. As if my life had stopped, and re-started somewhere else.

I was delivered to A&E. The medic spoke to a nurse:
'He's been knocked unconscious. Don't know how long for.'
Then he was gone. There was a long night of waiting for various tests. At 5 am June arrived to take me home. I was a bit knocked about, but no lasting harm. I cracked the old joke about having a brain scan and the medical staff being unable to find anything. June recalled the night's events:
'I wondered where you'd got to. Some lights pulled onto the drive. There was a policeman at the door. I didn't want to answer it.'
June watched too many crime programmes. Then wondered why she was so nervous at night.
It was almost daybreak when I got into bed. I slept like the dead.

The following lunchtime I emerged into the light and did a kit inspection. Everything was attached. Senses seemed to be working. Upper logic function seemed to be ok despite the headache. I had two large bumps around my temple. Cuts and grazes everywhere, and bruises emerging by the hour.
The police gave June an incident number. Using this I was able to get the phone number of the woman at the scene of the accident. I called her and thanked her for looking after me.
'Can you tell me what happened?'
She'd been queuing at a chip shop. Heard an almighty bang behind her and turned around to see me in the middle of the road with my bike on top of me. I wasn't moving. Then, in her own words:
'Please God be alive.'

It took me a moment to respond.
'How long was I unconscious for?'
'Probably half a minute? We dragged you off the road. Luckily a car stopped just in time.'
She continued to fill in the gaps in my memory. I'd been knocked off my bike by a pizza delivery van. He was in a rush, and had turned right without looking.
'He did come back and check you were alright though.'
I remembered the man's voice.
'I know him' she continued, 'Not very well mind, -the lift doesn't go all the way to the top floor with him.'
I could imagine her finger at her temple.
She laughed:
'Do you know what he said to the policeman?'
'Go on.'
'Can I go now mate? I've got a pizza to deliver!'
We laughed.
'The Police told him straight: "You're not going anywhere until we've sorted this out" -unbelievable!'
I thanked her again and said goodbye. I was really grateful for her help.

If you see a pizza delivery van with a dent in the passenger door, then let me know. I would like to congratulate him on his customer service. If your 11pm pizza wasn't quite as warm as it should have been on that evening back in May, then blame me. It's all my fault.

There was no chance of a successful prosecution. I couldn't remember anything, and the woman had her back to the incident. Weird how your memory can blot things out. I should have been able to remember the headlights coming towards me. The impact. Hitting the ground. I had been lucky this time. Very lucky. It was probably best not to rely on luck anymore. Maybe it was about to run out.

In July 2017, I was back at the doctor's with another urinary tract infection. Different doctor this time. One who appreciated that there might be an underlying cause. One quite happy to dismiss the notion that I was some kind of Sex God.
'It's unusual for a man to get a UTI because the urethra is so much longer than a woman's. Hmmm...'
He looked at my medical record.
'This is the second one in less than twelve months.'
He gave me some tablets and a little plastic urine sample bottle. No unwanted penetrations or prodding about. It was all going so well. I'd be straight out as fast as I came in.
Then he gave me a blood sample form.
'I'm going to ask for a PSA test.'
This, ladies and gentlemen, is how my little journey began.

Too embarrassed to confess my ignorance in front of the doctor, I rushed home to the internet and found out that PSA stands for 'Prostate Specific Antigen'. PSA is a protein produced by the prostate to assist in the manufacture of semen (which gives the sperm something to swim in). However, if the prostate is irritated, PSA can find its way into the bloodstream.
I popped into the surgery a few days later and gave a blood sample. My infection disappeared and I forgot everything I'd just learned on the internet. It was only of academic interest anyway. I doubt the question would come up in a pub quiz. I felt fine. Ignorance was bliss.

One morning, a month later, a letter dropped onto the mat. A letter for me. Not sure who from. No clues on the postmark. I was about to go to work. I usually just tossed mail on the kitchen table so I could open it later. Probably junk mail. A few letters from SAGA had arrived recently. They specialised in holidays and insurance for the elderly. I was on their radar. From their point of view, I was worth a little effort. Worth pursuing. I wouldn't be able to outrun them forever. Maybe it was one of those plans where for a fiver a month, you could get help with funeral costs. I was living life in the fast lane.

For some reason my curiosity was aroused.

The letter had 'NHS' at the top. I'd never had a letter from the NHS before. My eyes danced over the page. It was an appointment with a consultant urological surgeon no less. I was attracting some unwelcome interest.

'I've got an appointment on the fifth of September.'

June looked over my shoulder.

'Blimey -you should prepare to be in clinic for up to three hours.'

I tried to make light of it:

'I'd better take a packed lunch!'

'You need to arrive with a full bladder' she continued. 'Oh, and what's a DRE?'

'I don't know, but it looks like I might be having one.'

I was sure it would be fine. We were both keen supporters of our local football team, Cheltenham Town. We had plenty of experience of coping with disappointment and difficult times.

My first hospital waiting room. We had to squirt some antiseptic gel onto our hands and then we were in the Urology department. I tapped my name and date of birth onto a screen and checked myself in. My arrival flashed around the hospital. I imagined nurses abandoning half-made beds. Doctors grabbing stethoscopes -or whatever they grabbed these days and running down the corridors.

Investigations

Orderlies leaving trollies behind. All getting in each other's way as they rushed to Urology.

I looked around the waiting room. Hardly a stir. Heaps of clothes slumped on uncomfortable chairs. Maybe not a panic after all -my arrival had gone almost entirely unnoticed.

I took a seat. Tried to relax. I'd discovered that DRE stood for 'Digital Rectal Examination'. I was too worried to investigate further. Ignorance was bliss.

My engineering background interpreted this as a test that was done electronically. It had to be in this high-tech age surely? In my darker moments I imagined it might not be.

I looked around the waiting room. We were all a bit worn round the edges. Old age creeps up on you. There's no formal announcement. I figured 'youth' could be stretched up to your thirtieth birthday. 'Middle age' was elastic enough include whatever age I was currently at. 'Old age' was always a year or two in front of me, and 'elderly' could be postponed indefinitely.

A nurse popped her head round the door. Heads lifted out of magazines. A name. Not mine. Heads dropped back down.

The difference between young and old could be defined thus: If you were young, you 'fell over'. If someone says you've 'had a fall' then you have crossed the boundary into old age. At least in the eyes of other people. A young, ambitious, upwardly mobile person has a 'power nap'. Try saying you've had a 'power nap' to someone once you're over fifty. They will smile knowingly and say 'oh you mean a nap'. That's if they don't burst out laughing. Of course it's the same thing. Just a question of perception. There comes a point in life when a greeting like:

'Hi Dave -how are you hanging?'

Becomes:
'Hello Dave. You're looking well'.
Like they're surprised you're still alive.
Did you notice the boundary where you crossed into old age? Did you miss a few clues? Like the first time your hairdresser asked you if you wanted your eye-brows trimming? Like the arrival of your first bowel cancer screening kit?

Nurse again. Someone else. His shoulders slumped like an elk that had just been shot through the heart. Peace returned.

Only recently a girl offered her seat to me on a train.
A first.
I was philosophical about it. I just had to take her act of kindness in good heart. Accept it's a rite of passage. Naturally, for June's amusement, I looked over my shoulder as if she must surely have been addressing someone else. Of course, I knew she was talking to me.
Shortly afterwards the ticket collector came by. We paid our fare. I thought I'd given the exact money, but there was some change.
'Oh, that's not bad' I thought to myself. Must be a special offer.
I checked the stub. I'd been given a concessionary fare -without even asking. Fine if you qualify but a bit galling when your still five or six years away.
Two blows to my ego in one day. No, hold the front page, two blows *inside a minute*. I was having a particularly bad day. Maybe I should try that wrinkle-free cream June used, or skip the expense and go straight to Polyfilla.

Nurse again. Not me.

Old age has few advantages - you might as well take whatever benefits are on offer.

My private nightmare was insuring the car on-line. The bit where you entered your year of birth always caused a little anxiety. I'd scroll back through the years, back into the last century, back into the pre-Cambrian era. It was frightening how far back I had to scroll. I needed to allow a bit more time for this. It was a fearful indicator of how the years had passed. I have this worry that one day my year of birth won't be there at all, and I won't be able to get insured.

Nurse again. I check my letter to be sure I've got the right day.

Age is a completely different subject for a woman and is a potential minefield from a man's point of view. If a woman asks you how old you think she is, no answer should be attempted without a solicitor and first-aider present. In my experience you start by knocking ten years off your original estimate. Then another five if you ever want to talk to this woman again. Then another five for margin of error. The reality is, your guess can never be too low.

Names were called. Seats started to empty. Mine would have to be called soon. It was like a verbal version of Russian Roulette.

Yes! Here we go.
I was up on my feet. So **somebody** had registered my arrival. I moved inexorably towards my fate.

She was calm. Spoke quietly. It must be the first law of passing on bad news. Can you imagine the effect on the patient if the medical person starts flapping about? Looking flustered or even panicky? She looked like she had everything under control. I wish I did. Her calm demeanour translated itself to me. To both of us. Calmness was infectious. But then so was panic.

'Your PSA reading was 30.'

I let her do the talking -my voice might betray my anxiety.

'We prefer this to be under five, so this is a slight worry. It may be that your urinary tract infection has elevated your PSA levels.'

'Yes, that must be it' I thought to myself.

'We will get you to do another PSA test now the infection has cleared up. If this still shows elevated values we will investigate further.'

'F-further?'

'Yes. We will perform an ultrasound to check for retention. Also, an MRI scan and possibly a biopsy depending on results.'

While she spoke to me, she rolled her biro between her fingers. On my left I saw a floor-length curtain. What lay behind this curtain I could only guess at, but I suspected I was going to find out sooner rather than later. While she spoke I was quite calm, but when a drawer opened and some surgical gloves came out I knew my luck was about to run out. There was nothing electronic about what was going to happen next.

'I'm going to give you an internal examination.'

I was about to have a finger inserted into my back passage with the intention of examining my prostate. Part of me wanted to be thoroughly checked over. This was in conflict with the other part, which wanted to run as far as possible in the opposite direction. I remembered her long slender fingers fiddling with her pen. I supposed it could be worse. She could have been a man with fingers like tree trunks.

The curtains swished. As I thought - a bed. A woman was inviting me to climb onto it. I had never previously refused an offer like this, but something told me this would be memorable for a different reason.

How my world had changed. 'Old age doesn't come alone' someone once said to me.

My trousers came down. My medical record -or the sparseness of it, probably gave her a clue that I was a virgin in the DRE department. No one had ever been there. Not Ranulph Fiennes. Not even Captain James T Kirk. She was going to boldly go where no man had gone before. The biggest clue of all was my overwhelming look of dread.

'I'll be as gentle as I can Mr Meredith.'
That was genuinely re-assuring. There was a squirt of gel. I just closed my eyes and thought of England. Anything. Great Cheltenham Town performances. No good. Wouldn't last long enough.
I felt something near the exit door.
Think of something! Quick! 'The quick brown fox jumps over the lazy dog. Every good boy deserves favour -or was it frui..'
Oh God! She was in. I couldn't distract myself. It felt like she was feeling around for a sixpence at the back of the sofa. Bloody hell. Hurry up and find it. Something wriggling about inside me. Then she was out.
This had been my worst nightmare, but it hadn't been anything like as bad as I was expecting. Not something you'd do to cheer yourself up of course, but not so bad after all. Maybe I was just glad it was all over. I thought she might have to chisel her way in.
'Pop your clothes back on Mr Meredith.'
Dignity returned.
'It feels enlarged but fairly smooth' she said, as we returned to her desk.

'A rough surface or a hard lump might indicate a problem. This doesn't rule anything out of course.'

Maybe the one benefit of getting older is that your body gives way more easily. **Yields** more readily. I had a tooth extraction recently and marvelled at how easily the tooth came out. I related this to someone at work:

'Modern dentistry has really moved on' I enthused, 'years ago it would have been quite an ordeal to remove a molar.'

'It's nothing to do with advances in dentistry!' laughed my younger colleague:

'More likely your gums are receding due to age, and the teeth are beginning to fall out by themselves! Like rats deserting a sinking ship!'

At my place of work, they would conduct a 'lessons learnt' exercise if something unexpectedly went wrong. These were usually held in the main conference room, and I had attended more than was good for my career development. I remembered a slogan on the wall:

'The beauty of not planning, is that failure comes as a complete surprise and is not preceded by a period of anxiety and stress.'

You could say something similar about not following good medical advice. At the end of this book is a 'lessons learnt' summary, because learning lessons the hard way can be bad for your health. Like many people I have a 'bucket list' of things I want to do before I die. Most of my list consists of visits to faraway places, or taking a scissors to June's in-store credit card. Well, welcome to my alternative medical 'bucket list'. At the end of this book is a list of medical procedures (not exhaustive!) you are likely to undergo in your battle against prostate cancer. In my experience, the first time is always the worst because you don't know what to expect. If it's any comfort to you, there's really not a lot of actual pain involved, but your dignity will take a bit of a bashing. Unlike the usual 'bucket list' you shouldn't expect other people to cast envious eyes over it.

A letter dropped onto the mat. More unwelcome attention from the NHS. I was being invited in for a biopsy on the 11th November 2017 no less.

Ordinarily the prostate gland was in a difficult place from the point of view of obtaining a tissue sample. Fortunately, nature had thoughtfully provided a convenient inspection hole.

2. Biopsy

'Convenient' is an interesting word. What was 'convenient' for the medical team wouldn't necessarily be 'convenient' for me. Even with my limited anatomical knowledge I'd already worked out how these tissue samples were going to be obtained, and it wasn't going to be under a general anaesthetic. It seemed to be a flaw in the system. The urethra has to pass right through the middle of the prostate. Any swelling would immediately restrict the flow of urine from the bladder. If we had designed something similar at work, it would never have been signed off by the engineering team. Maybe nature didn't have a 'lessons learnt' session, although Charles Darwin was pretty sure it did.

The blissful ignorance that had served me so well was coming to a rude end. I was now 'Googling' frantically. Finding out what I could. Following my digital examination, I had been invited in for an MRI scan and an ultrasound scan. These had not taxed my limited reserves of bravery. If I was expecting some feedback on the results then I was going to be disappointed. They were like a team of detectives, secretly gathering overwhelming forensic evidence, before charging their hapless suspect. Maybe I'd find out more today.

We Found our way to the urology department and made our presence known.
'Ah Mr Meredith. Can you hang on a moment? The registrar wants a word.'
Soon we were being shown into a small office. Introductions were made and then we were down to business.
He was looking intently at the screen. I didn't like it when he did that. Something unexpected could be guaranteed and trying to

concentrate in these circumstances was like trying to knit fog. He had my undivided attention – not that it would help me much.
'I'm afraid that..'
Not a good start.
'..your ultrasound has revealed..'
Revealed what? His words came too quickly now.
'..that you have chronic retention.'
Was that something to do with memory?
'Your bladder is not draining properly. You appear to be carrying about 700ml of urine around with you. We'll have to keep you in overnight.'
'Oh.'
He looked at June:
'I know it's a bit unexpected but once we have performed the biopsy, will you be able to get your husband an overnight bag?'
My prostate had swollen to the point where it was choking my urethra – making it difficult to pass water. I had no idea. My flow wasn't what it was, but it was still reasonable. Ok I wasn't jet-washing a hole in the little blue toilet de-odouriser anymore, but I wasn't experiencing any discomfort either. No blood in the urine. He returned to the screen. More to come?
'Hmm. That probably explains the urinary tract infections. The problem is that a large volume of warm urine is an ideal breeding ground for viruses.'
Inch by inch they were building an overwhelming case for the prosecution. For the moment I was one step ahead of the law.

We joined a number of older men who all had their wives or family there for moral support.
We all knew what we were there for. Time ticked by. A nurse popped her head round the door. Then she disappeared.

'Blimey that was close' I thought to myself.
Everyone breathed a sigh of relief.
Calm was restored -for the moment.
A door opened. Everyone straightened up. Another nurse. She walked purposefully amongst us. If we'd any freedom of movement, we would have scattered like a flock of sheep. Was she going to tap someone on the shoulder? We recoiled away from her. Then she was gone.
'...and relax.' I thought to myself.
Then another head popped round the door:

'Mr so and so'

Some poor sod rose to his feet. It wasn't me. I watched the nurse smile and shepherd him into an adjoining room. The door closed. Something unpleasant was surely going on behind it. Ears strained but discovered nothing.

My gaze returned to my 'House and Home' magazine. I tried to read. I'd start a sentence but couldn't concentrate long enough to finish it. The articles were far too long, given that I didn't know whether I was waiting two hours or two minutes. In my fidgety state I needed shorter articles like 'how to switch a light on'.
I tried another magazine. I can't recall which one it was but it was clearly aimed at an older readership. Actually, an elderly readership. I wondered if its circulation was dwindling due to natural wastage.
The articles were shorter. I suppose they had to be, given their readers couldn't be sure how much time they had left. The articles all seemed to have a coloured drawing of an elderly couple looking

into a sunset. I couldn't concentrate on these either. I skipped to the classifieds. These might suit my attention span.
Walking frames. Oh gawd, a ridiculously healthy woman using a stair-lift. Funeral plans. And, -this was surely a joke -headstone cleaner.

The first man to be called returned to the waiting room. Eyes bored into him looking for clues. I scrutinised him from top to bottom. Especially bottom. He seemed to be walking normally. No damp patches. He was a bit older than me. I studied his face for clues.
His family stood up.
He looked tired. Drawn. Like an Arsenal supporter who has just watched his team lose to Spurs.
'You alright Dad? What was it like?'
Every man in the room discretely looked up from their magazines. The whole room was in suspense. Like he was about to give you the lottery numbers for the coming Saturday. All waited on his reply.
He gave a sigh:
'Well, that was....how do I put it……unforgettable.'
His words were analysed. Dissected. What did he mean by that? Unforgettable?
Unforgettable, like reclining on a chaise longue in some Greek Temple with only a fig leaf protecting your dignity. All the while, attendant nymphs dangle grapes, while others fan the scent of a hundred bee-orchids and sacrifice a virgin for your pleasure.
That kind of 'unforgettable'? Maybe not.

I was about to find out for myself. I made my way along a short corridor and was shown into a small room. I confess I don't remember much about the preamble. My memory was switched off. It was in safety mode, like the moments before that impact with the pizza van.

'Hello Mr Meredith.' Said the gathered group of medical staff. Introductions were made, but it would have been a miracle for me to have remembered anybody in those circumstances. I did my best to look some of them in the eye and say hello, but I couldn't get past the fact that every pair of eyes in that room were about to get intimately acquainted with my bottom. I didn't know where to look. I certainly didn't want my eyes settling on any of the medical equipment.

I tried to be bright and breezy, but it was hard given that I was about to lose any last remaining shreds of dignity. I felt disorientated. Helpless.

'Take your trousers and pants off for me and hop onto the bed.'

'Can you lean on your side facing away from me and draw your knees up to your stomach.'

'Ah the foetal position' I thought to myself. This was a familiar position for me. I adopted it whenever June was giving me a telling off.

'You're about to hear a large click. This is the sound the equipment makes when it takes a tissue sample. We aren't doing anything yet, we just want to make you familiar with the sound.'

There was a loud click. A bit like the trigger of an unloaded shotgun. Not that I was much of a firearms expert.

'As we take a sample the equipment anaesthetises the prostate. You shouldn't feel any pain.'

People moved into pre-arranged positions.

'We are about to start Mr Meredith. Are you comfortable?'

'I'm fine' I lied.

'We going to apply a little lubricating gel. It may feel a little cold.'
I felt a wet cloth. Then a spurting sound.
Then there was the sound of running water and latex being stretched.
A man's voice:
'I'm going to do a digital examination Mr Meredith. Are you ok?'
'I'm fine.'
This was the starter before the main course. I'd had this starter before. It wasn't so bad this time.
My eyes settled on a bit of flaky paint. I needed to distract myself. This bit of flaky paint was the only thing in my field of view. What distraction potential did it have? Probably not enough.
I tensed. Held my breath.
I felt something enter me. A man's finger -moving around.
Ohhh! My bit of flaky paint needed to be sanded down...maybe a coat of...
'That feels fine Mr Meredith.'
'We are about to start the procedure. Let me know if you feel any pain. Are you ready?'
'Yes.'
I tensed up. Held my breath. My buttocks clenched, ready to repel the invader.
'Try and relax Mr Meredith. Here we go.'
Yes..maybe a coat of sealer. Ohh!! Something pushing into me. Uhh!
It felt like the nozzle of a vacuum cleaner.
It seemed huge.
I could feel myself stretched around it.
It was being waggled around. It felt like my hips were being separated.

Biopsy

..Maybe not sealer. Ohh!! ..an undercoat would probably...Uhh! **Please God** hurry up.
Click!
I felt a little pinch from somewhere inside the other end of my body. The probe was withdrawn with a plopping sound. There was a tinkle of surgical instruments against stainless steel.
I exhaled, un-tensed.
I stretched my legs out. Propped myself up on my elbows.
'Not yet Mr Meredith. We've got eleven more to do.'
Eleven!

OH---MY---GOD

Twelve samples from something the size of a large walnut. There wouldn't be anything left!
I slumped back onto the bed. Foetal position. My bravery all used up.
I found my bit of flaky paint.
I tensed. Held my breath.
..undercoat and top coat should do..Ohhh!
Click!
Pinch. Breathe out. Un-tense. Beads of sweat now.
Out of the corner of my eye I could see a head move away. Then another rattle of surgical instruments.
The heads came back towards me again.
I tensed. Held my breath.
..should I use matt or satin? This was Ohhh!..important. It would..Uhh!
Click!
Withdraw. Plop. Exhale. Relax. Clatter of surgical instruments. Oh God. Why me?

'You're doing very well Mr Meredith.'
I could only nod now.
Repairing the flaky bit of paint wasn't doing it for me anymore. I had to think of something. Anything.
What country did it look like? I squinted.
In the corner of my eye the heads moved back towards me.
I tensed. Held my breath.
It was obvious now.. it looked like...Ohh!.. India..
Click!
Uhhh! Withdraw. Plop. Heads move away. Clatter of metal on metal.

I tried to think about my secret lover. In a reckless moment I'd confessed my innermost thoughts about Julia Bradbury to my sister. Unfortunately, she later betrayed my trust at a WH Smiths' book signing event, where Julia was promoting her new walking book. She revealed to Julia that I would happily drink her bathwater. So Julia knows my sordid secret. I've blown my chances with her now. The pain of my disappointment masks the discomfort long enough to get through two clicks. She probably showers anyway.

Heads moved back towards me. Oh God! They're coming back for more:
Tense! Hold breath. Ohh!
Click!
Breathe out.
I couldn't think of anything other than my bottom hole now. It wasn't so much that someone had gone in the wrong way through the exit door, more that the door might never close properly again. I couldn't distract myself from what was going on any longer.

Was that six or seven? Christ, I couldn't even count any more. I was damp with sweat.
I had to get through to the end.
'Mr Meredith. I have an assistant who would benefit from the experience of taking the last few samples.'
'Are you happy for her to proceed?'
'Christ!' I thought to myself. 'Why don't you poke your head into the waiting room and see if anyone else fancies a go while you're at it.'
'Sorry Mr Meredith – I didn't catch your reply.'
'Yes, that's perfectly fine' I croaked.
They counted down the last few.
'That was the last one Mr Meredith!'
I rolled slowly off the bed.
I was exhausted. But somehow elated. It was over.

As my clothes went on my dignity returned. I felt like a person again.

Then I thought to myself: There's probably only one thing worse than undergoing this and that was performing it. There was no way I would, or even could, have done it. At least I'd only seen a bit of flaky paint. They had witnessed something far worse. I thanked them all from the heart of my bottom.
There wasn't really any pain as such, it's just uncomfortable, undignified and unfamiliar. I suspected that the first time was always the worst, because at least with subsequent procedures you know what to expect. I took comfort from the fact that I had helped a trainee surgeon in the advancement of her career. You could say she was starting at the bottom and working her way up.

Biopsy

June had gone home to make me an overnight bag. I'd completely lost any sense of time. I didn't know whether I'd been in there for fifteen minutes or fifteen hours, but I was relieved that it was all over. I returned to the waiting room, which was almost empty. I sat near an elderly couple. One look at his face told me that he hadn't been in yet. Another name was called. Not him. He was going to be the last one in.
'I hope you don't mind me asking but are you here for a biopsy?'
They nodded.
I wanted to re-assure them. He'd had a long wait.
'I've just had mine.'
I had their full attention. Especially him. I leant forward.
'It's nothing to worry about. A bit undignified and...'
Just at that moment some lubricating gel made its way out of the back door. It was as much as I could do to stop some air following it out and ruining my calming effect.
'..Uh..a bit uncomfortable but ok.'

We chatted for a few minutes. He seemed re-assured. I was conscious of someone nearby:
'Mr Meredith?'
A nurse. I nodded and stood up.
'Would you like to come this way?'
Well actually I wouldn't if I'm brutally honest. I preferred the words 'You're free to go'.
'Sure'
I looked back at the couple.
'It's been nice talking to you.' My eyes met his: 'It'll be alright.'
'Thankyou' his wife replied.

'Come this way Mr Meredith —we're going to pop a catheter in.'
'Pop a catheter in'. The words came easily to her. I was particularly concerned about the word 'pop'. When I posted a letter, I 'popped' it in a letter box. It made no contact with the letter box as it went in, and if you listened carefully you could hear it flutter down on top of all the other mail. Something told me the adjective 'pop' was going to be wholly inadequate to describe what was about to happen to me.
I was shown to a bed. The curtains swished around.
'Can you take all your bottom half clothes off for me?'
'Er. You —you mean underwear as well?'
'Yes. Then pop yourself on the bed and pull a sheet over yourself.'

They left. I lay there waiting for someone to appear. Some heels could be heard outside. At first they sounded quite distant. Then they got louder and louder. The curtains swished again:
'Hello Mr Meredith. My names Emma. I've got student nurse Faye with me. She's going to pop the catheter in.'

Underneath the sheet my love-pump was waiting to be revealed to an unsuspecting world.
I looked down. I tried to give him some advice:
Try and look impressive. Not **too** impressive you understand. That would be **mortifyingly embarrassing**. Without any fanfare or dry ice, without even a drum roll, my rocket launcher was about to be introduced to the nursing profession. The whole of this girl's education and training was simply a preparation for this moment. Would anything in this young girl's previous work experience have prepared her for what she was about to encounter? Maybe some experience with a fireman's hose? Some time with a tree surgeon? Would she crack under pressure? Would she turn and run out of

the hospital in floods of tears, her nursing career over before it had really begun?

The sheet was pulled back.
Oh gawd. What was the expression June used? Walnut Whip?
I was hoping for some raised eyebrows. Maybe even a step back. A low whistle of approval. Possibly even a call for back-up. Reality hit me: I could tell without even looking that this young woman was able to restrain wonder-weapon between her thumb and forefinger.

Under the supervision of the more experienced nurse, her junior partner applied an antiseptic wipe.
'Not too unpleasant so far' I thought to myself.
Under normal circumstances this would have been enough to bring the rocket into firing position, but the appearance of a plastic syringe loaded with lubricating gel was enough to make the control room abort the launch. There was a desperate attempt to withdraw the weapon back into its underground silo.
The last time I'd seen a nozzle like that was in B&Q when I needed to re-apply the mastic around the bath. I thought she might squirt a blob on the end, but the angle of attack suggested otherwise. There was going to be a head-on collision. There could be only one winner.
'I'm just going to apply some lubricating gel Mr Meredith. This might feel a little cold'.
I always prided myself on being my ability to compromise. To be accommodating when the situation demanded it but..
...surely that wasn't going to fit in there?
She made an opening and pushed the plunger in.
Oooh!'

I tensed. It was withdrawn. I breathed out. I had an awful feeling that there was more to come. I made a feeble joke:
'Is that it then?'
The nurses smiled at each other. Then there was the sound of a plastic bag being opened up. Then I caught sight of my first catheter. It looked like something you might water the garden with. There was no point in protesting. It had been a long day and I promised myself this was the final hurdle. I couldn't look. My eyes settled on the forearm of the student nurse.

'Oooh!'
My heels pressed into the mattress. This was crossing the threshold between uncomfortableness and pain. I held my breath. My urethra had always been a one-way street as far as traffic was concerned. Nothing had ever tried to go the wrong way. This was like an articulated lorry going the wrong way up a one-way street, and being so wide it was taking all the shop windows with it.
'Oh…Oh…Oh..Oooohh!'
My hand instinctively touched her forearm. My bravery levels hadn't recovered from the biopsy.
'Give me a little cough Mr Meredith.'
There was a final lunge of the 'artic' then it came to rest. It stopped moving. I closed my eyes and breathed out. They got busy with another syringe. This one looked like it was full of water.
'Almost finished Mr Meredith.'
There was a strange feeling from somewhere low down.
'Oooh!'
'You did pretty well Mr Meredith'.
I was damned sure I hadn't, but I was happy to accept praise from any quarter.

They propped me up a bit so I could see what was going on. It wasn't a pretty sight. They were fitting a bag to the end of my tube.
'Which leg do you want me to fit it on Mr Meredith?'
I was puzzled. Then it started to make sense. Think about being measured for a suit.
'Which side do you dress sir?'
'Bro, which way do you hang -your thang?!'
I touched a leg. Sorry dear reader. You should be shielded from such intimate information -I've revealed enough already. I looked down at myself. I was a sorry sight. The rocket which had so often pointed skywards now conformed to a more modest trajectory, uselessly following the catheter down my leg.
I wondered how long it would be out of action.
Then they were gone.

Shortly another nurse arrived. She checked the bag. The 700ml of urine I had been carrying around for so long, was now filling the bag up nicely. I looked at the positives: I'd just lost a pound and a half in weight without even trying. Permanently. A slightly drastic way of winning yourself a 'slimmer of the day' certificate if you ask me.

The nurse explained the function of the catheter. Fundamentally it was a tube that passed along the urethra, through the middle of the prostate and up into the bladder. At the bladder end was a water-filled balloon that prevented the catheter from coming out of the bladder. This was inflated after fitting using a water-filled syringe. This was inserted into a little valve which existed just at the point where the catheter left the body. The other end of the catheter was fitted into a plastic bag which was strapped to my leg. This had to be regularly checked, and I was to empty it if full.

High up on my thigh was a 'statlock'. A rotating clip which secured the tube to my leg. This was an important bit of kit because it prevented the catheter from being accidentally tugged or pulled and causing a problem with the water filled balloon in the bladder. The bag had to be changed at bedtime for a 'bed bag' which hung on a plastic frame by the bed. This had a sufficiently larger capacity that it enabled you to get right through the night without having to empty it. Both the leg-bag and bed-bag had to be replaced weekly, to guard against infection. I had been fitted with a 28 day catheter which would have to be replaced after this time by a 3 month catheter. I was to contact the district nurse to get the catheter changed.

There. I had my answer: It would be some time before my rocket would ever prepare for launch again. There would be no more space exploration. Not for the time being. Not until the cause of my 'chronic retention' had been treated.
I would receive a delivery of medical supplies in the next few days. I needed to empty the bed-bag first thing in the morning, and switch to a leg bag for the day ahead. I was to drink plenty of water to guard against blockage of the catheter, and if there was no sign of flow into the bag, I was to get medical assistance.
It was a lot of information to take in. My brain was full. What once took place automatically and without much thought, would now have to be managed. Up until now it had been enough to just respond to a call of nature and point Percy in the right direction. Now it was a constant worry.
'I'm sorry Mr Meredith but your urine retention has put a strain on your kidneys. The catheter will allow your kidneys to function normally. I'll be back in a moment to take a blood sample so we can see if your kidney function is back to normal.'

Later June arrived with my overnight bag. My happiness at her appearance took me my surprise. I tried to be cool. I welcomed her in the most manly and gruff voice I could. Not wanting to show how pleased I was to see her. Silly mannish behaviour. It was a relief to see her familiar face. Mainly because her behaviour was more predictable. She wasn't about to push some pointy thing into me without warning. Generally, if she was going to cause me grievous bodily harm, there were usually clear warning signs. I had learned not to ignore them. Tight lips, folded arms and the words 'that's fine' said between gritted teeth, meant things were definitely not 'fine' and I was expected to make a change of course fairly rapidly. She brought me familiar objects. A book I had been reading. A classic car magazine. My old pyjamas. And grapes -of course. Things that gave my strange surroundings a little flavour of home.

We were both worried about the way the biopsy appointment had turned into an overnight stay.
She tried to lighten the mood. She lifted my sheet.
'Alright then Big Dick?'
I smiled. Everything would be ok. All too soon she was gone. The ward was prepared for the night. A nurse changed me into my bed bag. It became surprisingly quiet.

I hardly moved during the night. I didn't know how robust this catheter was. I was frightened I might disturb it. Needless to say, I didn't sleep that well. I dreamt of the bag being full to bursting and urine filling my mouth.

With the presence of the catheter there would be a new waking routine. Normally the first thing I did upon waking was apologise to

June, but in her absence the catheter got my full attention. There would be a sigh of relief if full. This meant that no blockage had occurred. A second sigh if the urine was a nice 'straw' colour. Then a sigh of relief that I had woken at all. I became intimately involved with the workings of my urinary system. Later June arrived to see how I was getting on. By late afternoon my kidney function result was deemed satisfactory, and I heard the magic words:
'You're free to go.'

I got home and read the leaflet: 'Living with an indwelling catheter'. I realised I would be dependent on this for some time. It would only disappear following an operation.
At this moment in time I assumed once the biopsy results showed I was clear of cancer, I would have a local operation to open out the urethra in the region of the prostate. This would allow urine to flow, and cure my chronic retention. This was the end of my sex life for the time being. What was once a threat to the entire female half of the population, was now nothing more than a diagnostic port.
But wait!
'Sex with an indwelling catheter.'
There was hope! I read the leaflet really carefully now:
'Before sex, a man can fold the catheter back alongside the shaft of the penis and tape it in place. A condom can then be applied over the penis and catheter.'
I was flabbergasted. These were surely the words of some over-enthusiastic salesman?
This wasn't a paper straw we were talking about here. The catheter tube was fairly rigid. It would have to be formed into a loop before I could tape it to my 'shaft'. And I'd have to maintain a certain level

of interest, or I'd have nothing to tape the catheter to. I bet there wasn't a video on YouTube.

I could see it now. A candlelit meal. Fine wine. Sparkling conversation. Then holding hands across the table and long lingering looks of love. That moment when nobody else exists. That moment when you both want to take the relationship to the next level. When knowing looks explode into smouldering passion.

In my current state I'd be checking my pocket for a condom and then, anticipating the moment, she'd seductively slide a roll of Gaffa tape across the table.

I wasn't even going to try and persuade June to do this. Not even to create a money-making YouTube video. This would definitely be a 'lights out' moment if I was going to try this at home. I would have to cradle her head in my arm and whisper the magic words. Trouble is I'd never found out what they were. It's time to break marital confidentiality here and tell you that June likes me to talk to her in French at moments like these. Not that she understands any French -she just thinks it sounds sexy. I look into her eyes, deep into her soul, and try my usual line:

'Mon cheri. Je dois me souvenir de mettre la poubelle demain.'[*]

That simply wouldn't work this time. I would have to use my best lines:

'Darling, I'm going to make love to you like no man has ever done before.'

Well what's wrong with that? It was undeniably true.

---

[*] 'My darling, I must remember to put the bin out tomorrow.'

Then somehow, with my free arm, work the scissors, tape, condom and catheter so deftly and seductively that she would find me irresistible.

'What was it like for you darling?' I daren't ask.

There was one benefit I suppose. No risk of passing on a sexually transmitted disease. In fact, no risk of passing on anything. I wondered what other household tasks I could perform while I was at it. Perhaps I could unblock that drain under the sink.

3 The Catheters Years Part 1

Less than two weeks into my 28-day catheter, there was a change in my waking routine. There was no sigh of relief on seeing a full bed-bag. That was because there was nothing in it. There was clearly a problem.
I checked the tap. Closed.
Felt the floor. Dry.
I sighed. I would have preferred a hefty carpet cleaning bill rather than cope with the only other likely cause which was a blocked catheter.

I couldn't default to my usual response of waiting a day or two to see if it got better by itself. Or maybe taking some aspirin. Or applying a sticking plaster and ignoring it altogether. It was time for action. Even I could see that. I didn't know what the medics did in these situations. I had no choice but to find out. I didn't think it warranted a visit to A&E so I decided to go to my local doctor's surgery.

I approached the receptionist. Suddenly a baby started crying nearby.
'Sorry Mr Meredith, you'll have to speak up.'
'I said, I think my..'
Just at that second the baby stopped crying as suddenly as it started. The word 'catheter' boomed around the waiting room before I was able to throttle back the volume control.
She smiled:
'Ok Mr Meredith. I'll get you into a Doctor as soon as I can.'
She was as good as her word. As soon as I arrived, the doctor phoned the district nurse so that by the time I was stretched out

on the bed, there was a knock at the doctor's door. Then a swish of curtains and a man at my bedside.

What on earth did this chap want? I realised I was in the presence of a **male** nurse. I didn't think I could get any more embarrassed than I was at this moment, but his presence meant I was about to be handled, intimately – by a man. Another addition to my bucket list. This was no time to be choosy. My bladder was insisting on some attention right away -if you don't mind. There wasn't time for interviews.

My catheter had a valve which enabled water to be pumped up the catheter and into the bladder to clear a blockage. This was known in the trade as 'flushing'. This was tried without success. No one was more disappointed than me, because now the whole lot would have to come out. With the benefit of experience, I learned that nurses all do this in different ways. Some pull with alternate hands like they're hauling a sail down on a boat. Getting a catheter out quickly for these guys is a task usually performed against a stop watch. You'd think there was an Olympic Games qualifying time. It's a matter of personal pride. Something they might boast about at the end of their shift.
For others, the catheter tube is held delicately between the thumb and forefinger like you would hold the stem of a rose. It was caressed. Spoken to. Tempted out of hiding. Pulled so gently, that it almost fell under its own weight. It came out in stages. When it felt like it – the nurses pausing for a cup of tea at regular intervals.

A syringe was fitted to the valve. Water was drawn out of the balloon. The speed at which this was performed suggested that we were about to witness something special. An attempt at the catheter withdrawal world record. I suppose I should have been honoured to have played a supporting role.

I remembered the way I buckled when the thing had gone in. This had been performed by a female nurse, and somehow the embarrassment of my pathetic whimpering was easier to bear in front of a woman. In front of a male nurse I had no alternative but to tough it out. I couldn't appear to be weak in front of another man. No good asking him to be gentle with me. The very thought invited mockery. I was tempted to say something in a workmanlike tone such as:
'Yeah, just whip it out'.
But I suspected no further encouragement was necessary. He reached for the catheter. The doctor peered over his shoulder. He looked like he was adjusting his watch.
I reminded myself that I was in a doctor's surgery. An ideal place if too much enthusiasm was displayed. I guessed that if the whole of my lower intestines came out, the attempt would be rendered null and void.
'Uuuh!'
An electric shock started somewhere deep inside my abdomen and shot along my urethra to the tip of my penis.
They must have heard me in the waiting room. My eyes watered. I felt like I'd just been pulled off a skewer. This was my finest hour. I managed some words. A barely audible whisper:
'I have to say that was a lot easier than I expected.'

No urine flowed. Even with the catheter out of the way. In the short time I'd been wearing the catheter, my urethra had relaxed. With the catheter gone the pressure from the swollen prostate was enough to close it completely.

Wonder-weapon was treated to an antiseptic wipe and a plunger filled with lubricating gel. Strange to record that it wasn't so bad this time. I suppose after accommodating a garden hose, a little syringe was now nothing to worry about. Then the new catheter was offered up. Bladder really complaining now. My knees wanted to come up. My hands wanted to press on my lower abdomen.

It was going in. Like firemen entering a burning building. Two overbearing discomforts battled for possession of my nervous system. My bladder was just ahead on the judge's scorecard. Ahead to the extent that the catheter was going in almost unnoticed. If you can believe such a thing. Then the balloon was inflated. The bag attached.

Silence in the surgery.

Anxious looks further down the bed.

'Just seeing if it's filling Mr Meredith.'

You expected the urine to come out like a geyser, blowing the bag off your leg. But it doesn't -despite the pressure on your bladder. It will empty in its own time. If that's alright with you.

Seconds tick by. I noticed the clock in the surgery. Calm words:

'It's flowing. Filling up slowly.'

I breathed out. Completely emptying my lungs for the first time in ages. Relief. Aching going away.

'Thanks'.

'No problem. I had to move quickly there.'

Despite the discomfort, I was glad he did. I didn't want urine backing up into the kidneys and causing problems there.

Calm was restored. I had a question to ask:

'That catheter seemed to go in without too much problem?'

'I'm not surprised. The hospital fitted a size 16 catheter. Too large in this case. They are used in situations where blood clots or debris have to be able to pass out of the bladder. I've fitted a size 14. You should find this more comfortable.'

I was all back to normal. Well, as normal as you can be with a tube sticking out of your body. At one time I would have recoiled at the thought of another man fiddling with my wonder-weapon, but I just realised this was another tick on my bucket list. After thanking him I took the opportunity to ask him some questions.
'What caused my blockage?'
He shrugged his shoulders.
'Sometimes a urinary tract infection. Sometimes not drinking enough water. Sometimes it's – how do I put this - nocturnal activities?'

I knew my collar size, shoe size and inside leg. To that list of intimate measurements, I could now add a new one. Catheter size. Fourteen. If anyone in the medical profession is reading, then I would just like to say that my preferred catheter withdrawal speed is slow. Dead slow. No record attempts thank you.
Just the previous night we'd watched a reality TV show. One of the contestants displayed some of her tattoos. There was one at the base of her back: 'reload'. We groaned. A bit tasteless. It got me thinking about a tattoo. I remembered soldiers having their blood group tattooed on their body in case they were badly wounded. My tattoo would be at the top of my leg. I wasn't going to leave anything to chance. Just a few words. Something that reflected my stage in life:
'Cath. Size 14 SLOW.'

It was around this time that I started to make a dolls house for my granddaughter. It would take my mind off the interminable wait between the various stages of my treatment. Not just any old dolls house though. This was going to be a one-twelfth scale replica of the house she lived in. I'd got a few photos of the house already, and by counting the number of bricks I could make a pretty good guess at its dimensions. I drew some plans up, but I couldn't get the proportions to match the photos. It was a large Edwardian house with an in-and-out drive, but I soon realised where my problem was. My brick dimensions were based on modern sizes. I needed to know the actual brick size and mortar thickness. It was intended to be a surprise, to both my daughter and granddaughter, so there was no question of simply asking. There was no alternative but to make a clandestine visit with a rule. I couldn't risk being discovered in the act, so I planned my visit for early in the evening. Enough light to see what I was doing, but dark enough for the household lighting to give me an indication of what rooms were being occupied at that moment.

I parked at a discrete distance and crept up the drive as casually as I could. Unfortunately, as I placed my rule against the brickwork, I was conscious of being watched. A dog walker had paused across the road. He must have seen me walk up the drive without making contact with the householder. I must have looked pretty suspicious. I was thinking neighbourhood watch. Or worse, a call to the police. I scribbled my dimensions down as quickly as I could.
I could allay his suspicions by approaching the front door, but that was simply out of the question. Every second here increased my chances of discovery, and the awkward questions that might follow. I walked down the drive towards him, turned left onto the

pavement, and threw a smile in his direction. There was no acknowledgment. I was gone.

Brick wallpaper had been ordered, various sizes of wood moulding and ply had been purchased. It was progressing well. I fed the new brick size into my plan and suddenly everything looked right.

'How much have you spent this time?' asked June as I came home after another visit to Hobbycraft.

'It was all on offer.' I lied.

She gave a dismissive shrug:

'You mean they gave you bits of wood and you offered money! That kind of offer!'

'The balsa was fifty pence a sheet, but two sheets for a pound! I couldn't turn that down!'

'It would be cheaper to actually buy the real thing.' she sniffed.

I turned the conservatory into a workshop. The light was good, and I could work in comfort. I was now old enough to listen to Radio 4. Two weeks of waiting for news had elapsed since my catheter emergency. At least my dolls house was progressing well even if my treatment wasn't. I was making good progress. I'd spent the whole of a rainy day in there, and June was keeping me supplied with cups of tea and food from the kitchen. I dropped a bit of wood moulding on the floor, and as I reached down to pick it up, I brushed against my lower leg. A thought occurred to me. I lifted up my trouser leg and looked at the catheter bag. Empty.

It was 6pm. A cold sweat broke over me. I'd been so pre-occupied all day that I'd completely forgotten about it.

I looked at the empty tea cup. I'd just drunk this and many others, and there was no evidence of any passage of fluid through my body. Where was all this tea going? June came into the conservatory.

'Another cup of tea?'
I didn't look up.
'Is everything ok?'
'I'm not sure. This bag should be full. I put it on first thing this morning, but I can't recall emptying it since then. I'd better not drink anymore.'

An hour went by. Then I had a feeling that I hadn't experienced for some time. The urge to go for a pee. This wasn't a feeling you should get with an in-dwelling catheter, because the urine simply passes from the bladder, through the catheter and into the bag. It was the sole advantage of having one. You were never interrupted by your bladder -you emptied the bag at your convenience. A dedicated couch-potato would see the benefits straight away. Uninterrupted TV viewing while the bag was hooked over the side of the loo. Anyway. I digress. I discussed my current predicament with June. There was no doubt now. I had a blocked catheter. The discomfort went away. I wasn't sure what to do.

'You'll have to go to hospital!'
'I feel alright at the moment. Maybe I should try and get through the night and go in the morning. It might start flowing again.'
Typical man response.
'Well it's up to you I suppose.'
I really didn't want to inconvenience anyone. Crazy really. I heard the scare stories on the telly about overstretched hospital resources. I didn't want to add to their burden. I was a man. I could cope. I remembered reading somewhere that it wasn't unusual for someone to go all day without having a pee. It wasn't something I'd ever paid much attention to. I didn't have a spreadsheet set up for it: 'Hey chaps – one and a half litres today!'

I kept leaning forward and straightening back up. My hands pressed into my groin. Like the abnormal repetitive behaviour of a polar bear in a zoo enclosure. We were on our way to A&E. Another first for me. Another thing to be ticked off my bucket list. The urge to pee had returned with a vengeance. There was an incapacitating feeling of discomfort.

We drove past the hospital. Yellow lines. June scanned the horizon looking for a space.

'I can't park on yellows.'

'What are you worrying about that for? Just abandon the f*cking thing!'

June spoke on my behalf at the reception desk. I was well past that. I paced up and down the waiting room. I couldn't settle. I kept clenching my buttocks. My back was damp with cold sweat. I'd crease up. Then sit down. Then stand up and read a notice. The words were all blurred. I became tearful. There were a few sideways glances in my direction. Maybe they thought I was trying to jump the queue. If anyone from Hollywood had been there, they would have recognised an Oscar winning performance – except it was frighteningly real.

'David Meredith?'

I stumbled past the others patiently waiting their turn. I found myself in front of a nurse. Help was at hand. The sight of her uniform made me tearful again. It required an incredible effort to compose myself to the point where I could get some words out. If I could force the words out, help would come. My distress was obvious. I lifted my trouser leg.

'E-e-empty all day. B-b-blocked' I stammered.

Relief. I'd got the words out. Then she was gone.

They wasted no time trying to flush the catheter. They were taking it straight out. A new one was going in. Any discomfort during the exchange was masked by the pain of my blockage. I looked down. Urine was flowing.
I covered my eyes: 'Oh thank God'.
The bag filled and filled – and filled some more. Another nurse had arrived. They exchanged glances.

It was unbelievably re-assuring to see my new bag slowly filling up. But I was also reminded at how helplessly dependant I now was on this tube of plastic. I was sat with a doctor being given antibiotics. Then she asked me to roll up my sleeve in readiness for an injection. 'Sometimes urine backs up into the Kidneys. This can cause kidney damage. We need a blood sample to check for this. I'm not expecting any problems – this is just precautionary.'

Soon June was driving me home. It was gone midnight. The roads were quiet.
'Sorry about the way I spoke to you. I was in a bit of a state.'
She just looked at me and smiled.
'Why don't we have a weekend away? I've found a little cottage in Dorset.'
We'd done this several times in the past. I'd always check to make sure there was a pub within walking distance so I could have a pint. Maybe some nice walks close by. Now there was another requirement:
'How far is it away from the nearest 24 hour A&E?'

4. Results

The new year started ominously. An appointment on January 2nd 2018 with a consultant urological surgeon to discuss the results of my biopsy. This was just routine. It would all be fine. I would get the 'all clear' and then have a local operation to open up my urethra. Not there and then -obviously.

Another waiting room. I looked discretely at all the faces gathered there. They were just ordinary people. Some looked quite well dressed. Others not so much. Illness is a great leveller. Most of the men were accompanied by their wives. Magazines were lifted up and put back down. Breathe was exhaled. Men were lost in their thoughts, pondering what the next hour would bring. Maybe some words of hope. Medical words. Words they never expected to hear. A door opened. A couple walked out. I recognised them. They were the couple I'd spoken to at my biopsy. They walked towards me, heading for the exit. He looked deep in thought. She caught my eye. Recognised me. We both smiled, and as she passed me she threw me a glance and mouthed the words 'Good luck'.

The time of my appointment crept ever closer. I would be called soon. I wondered what fate had in store for me. I thought about all the good health advice I'd been given over the years. The fibs I had told at 'well man' checks. The well-meaning advice I'd been given by the nurse at the doctor's surgery. Never mind about them. What had *I* done to improve my chances when the going got tough? My health couldn't entirely be the responsibility of the medical profession. Surely, I had to take some responsibility for it too? I looked up. I hoped my guardian angel was looking out for me.

Results

I'd been **reasonably** good. I'd brushed my teeth every day and had never smoked. That had to count for **something**. In my imagination I drew up a medical balance sheet. I had never smoked. That must put me ten points in credit.

A nurse popped her head round the door. Heads rose. A name was called. Not me. Someone over the far side. Back to my balance sheet.

I'd brushed my teeth **every** day. Ok nothing spectacular, but I needed my credit balance to be as good as possible before I started looking at the debits. Maybe a point. I had run three times a week for over thirty years. I once calculated the total distance to be over 25,000 miles. I was **still** running - even now. This was my ace card. What do you think? Twenty points? I had never carried any weight. Maybe another ten? Now I was struggling on the credit side.

The nurse again. Heads rose. Someone on the end of my row. Back to where I was.

I was scratching around for credits. I had always bent from the knees when picking something up. Not bending from the waist. Ok! Ok! I know what you're thinking: 'he's getting bit desperate now.' Let's look at the debits.
If I was playing skittles, I liked a drink. It's time to be honest now. Five pints. It wasn't my fault. I played my very best in between my fourth and fifth pints. Enough drink to relax properly, but not so much that I needed a compass to aim properly. I was doing this for the team -not me you understand. What shall we say: five points in the debit column? Come on -be nice to me!

I was married. It must make a difference. Trouble is I wasn't sure which column to put it in. I didn't want to get into trouble: ten in each.

The nurse again. A name. Getting close -someone opposite me. I looked beyond the nurse into the distant corridor. There was nothing unusual about this corridor. A few scuff marks on the wall. Maybe there'd been a scuffle – someone putting up resistance. Lives were being re-evaluated down there. Horizons were diminishing.

I supported Cheltenham Town football club. They were in danger of being relegated. They had sacked two managers already. They were having the kind of season where the stewards threw people **into** the ground, not **out** of the ground. I'd shout at the referee. Get worked up. This could not be good for my health. Thankfully this question never came up in my 'Well man' check. Ten points on the debit column.

Another name called. The guy next to me took the bullet. That was close! He looked like a bag of old clothes. He breathed out a tired breath and shuffled to his fate. I was going to present this balance sheet as a counter argument if things went badly. I needed to get it done. Press on.

I had a long-term problem with chocolate. It was attracted to me. One evening long ago, my children left their partially eaten Easter eggs on the dining table and went to bed. By the morning I'd eaten them all. To begin with I'd broken a little bit off each one. Then a bit more. Then I couldn't stop. There was an explosion of foil wrapper and bits of cardboard. At daybreak I had to sprint down to the shops to replace them before they woke up. They thought I was the best thing since sliced bread -they couldn't know the truth. I could hear a sweet paper wrapper at 500 metres. Hopeless case. Twenty point on the debit sheet.

Oh God! My name!
In that moment of standing up, there was a sudden realisation that this might not be just another routine appointment. My optimism melted away. My shoulders slumped to the point where I took on the shape of a charity clothes bag. June picked up her handbag. The nurse smiled. It was my turn in the corridor. My balance sheet evaporated in this tough new reality. I wasn't taking anything in. My head was swimming. In a matter of seconds, I was shuffling along like everyone else had been, my sparkle gone. The corridor was like a magnolia version of a hedge maze. I turned this way and that, like a rudderless ship. Then I was sat down in a little office. A door closed behind me. What was I doing here? Why me? Surely there was some mistake. Try and look relaxed.

'Please take a seat Mr Meredith.'

She spoke calmly. There was no drum roll. No fanfare. No dry ice. In the days when a judge was about to hand out the death-sentence, he would put a black cap on. There was no such clue today. On the telly the spectacles might be ceremoniously moved down the nose, and the hapless patient fixed by a pair of beady eyes. Not that either.
We could have been discussing my car's latest MOT failure. She cut to the quick:

'Of the twelve samples that were taken, four have been found to be cancerous.'

Her face seemed to retreat away from me down a long dark tube. I looked down on this poor chap trying desperately to hang on to the words pouring past his ears. He needed to take some of them home with him.
'Oy! You! Pay attention. She's talking to you!' I screamed down at him.

Then I was back looking at the consultant again. I was giddy with shock. Was there some mistake? She was still talking about me. Her voice seemed to come from another galaxy:
'T3a.'
'Gleason Scale seven, -three plus four.'
'Breaking out of the capsule.'
Bang. Bang. Bang. I nodded like I understood what was being said, but the reality was that I was drowning in words. I came up for air. I heard the word 'treatable'.
I clung on to it like a drowning man.
'T-treatable?' I spluttered.
'You have two choices.'

She showed me a diagram of medical places I didn't even know existed. Organs with strange names. Organs that had worked quietly in the background for over half a century. Organs that had now decided to go on strike. 'Down tools' took on a whole new meaning. I hardly knew anything about what my prostate did. She moved her pen around the diagram. It soon became obvious that it did perform a few handy functions. More than that -it was pretty much running the show down there.

'You can have a combination of hormones to shrink the prostate followed by radiotherapy to kill the cancer cells.'
'Or?'
'I've spoken to the surgeon and he is willing to perform a prostatectomy.'

By now I knew the implications of this operation. No ejaculation. No erection. A bit like cutting the rope on a hoist. I remember being incredulous that the removal option was only available at the discretion of the surgeon. I just assumed it would be offered to everybody. I looked at June. I suppose I should have asked her opinion, but at that moment it was my body. My decision. I didn't have to think twice:

'My father died of Prostate Cancer. I want to have it removed.'

'Oh, I see. Well you don't have to decide today. There will be a further appointment when you can inform us of your choice. Here is a leaflet which describes your options in more detail.'
I'd never been in hospital before. My ambition had been to live in perfect health until the age of 100, and then be killed by a jealous husband. I went into hospital to visit other people, never thinking I would be the one receiving the grapes. Mortality was knocking at my door.

'Before we can consider a prostatectomy you have to undergo a bone scan. This is to make sure the cancer hasn't spread to surrounding bone and tissue.'

The words 'breaking out of the capsule' came to mind. I tried to stay calm. My father's prostate cancer had been discovered too late. By the time of his bone scan it had already spread beyond the prostate into his pelvis and other bones. I remembered him complaining about his bad back.

'If you don't get past the bone scan then..' her voice tailed away.
'…It will just be hormone therapy.'

You'll know, if you've ever had a discussion like this, that all you want in the whole wide world is re-assurance. That with one wave of her magic wand, she will make it all go away. Failing that, she will turn the clock back a few hours, to a point when you hardly had a care in the world. But she can't, and you know it would be utterly foolish and unprofessional for her to offer false hope. At least this side of a bone scan. I was too shocked to ask questions, but the implications were clear. I had to have this bone scan as soon as possible. And I'd have to pass in order to progress to the next stage. I knew what failing the bone scan meant –that hormone therapy would do no more than hold back the inevitable. I would be looking at the 'managed exit'.

So there it was. The 'C' word had been used for the first time. It had crawled out from under its stone. It had always been a possibility – especially with the medical staff – but it had never really occurred to me. It was a complete shock. I'd been in total denial. I'd just gone along for the ride – expecting Thelma and Louise to drop me at the nearest bus stop before accelerating over the cliff. Naively I thought it might just have been a swelling. At worst a 'benign swelling'. What on earth **had I** been thinking about? The whole direction of travel had this outcome as its likely goal. How did I imagine it would be any different for me? Someone 'medical' has

Results

linked your name with the 'C' word and they don't do practical jokes.

The appointment was over. I couldn't even find the door. The whole episode had been so disorientating. Had I been on my own I would still be walking the corridors now. June had to lead me out of the building and repeat most of what the consultant had said. It was as if I hadn't really been there.

I was studying the booklet she gave me. It was a general-purpose booklet explaining the procedures around prostate cancer. There were some gaps where she had inserted values that were specific to my case. **My** values. This standard issue booklet was now personal.
There was a page detailing my Biopsy results.
It was a long time before I could look properly at this page. In fact, I'd get to this page in the book and have to put it down. I thought I might be able to leave it on a bus. Maybe if someone else picked it up it would become ***their*** problem. Here are my values:

Gleason score: 7 (3 +4)
The Gleason score is an indicator of how aggressive your cancer is and how fast the cancer cells are growing. Cancer cells are graded from 3 to 5 and low is good. 'Good' being a relative word of course. The score was made up of two numbers. The first number was a score for the ***majority*** of the cells seen on the biopsy result while the second number reflected the ***minority*** of cells.
If the cancer cells were consistent across all the biopsy samples then both the numbers would be the same. Hence a score of seven might be better for one person than another, depending on

whether the 4 came first or second. Hence the lowest overall Gleason score is 6. The highest 10.

T stage: T3a
The 'T' stage indicates how far the cancer has spread around the prostate. In my case the cancer was beginning to break out through the outer layer of the prostate. My cancer was 'Locally advanced'. Not good.

N stage: 'N0'
Cancer has not spread to the lymph nodes. Relief all round.

M stage:
'Awaited'.
The big unknown. Has the cancer spread to surrounding organs, such as the bones?
'Awaited' meant that this question could only be answered with a bone scan. Maybe not quite 'relief all round'.

I'm back home –deep in thought. It's disappointing to discover that there's nothing particularly special about my case. It's special to me - naturally, but I'm one of approximately 47,000 men who will be diagnosed in the UK this year. Of course, knowing that I had every intention of living forever, I expect shocked journalists from 'The Lancet' to camp outside my door. A peep out of the window shows only next-door's cat on its regular patrol. You expect the world to stop and take notice, but I only have the bog-standard variety of cancer and it will respond, or not, just the same as everyone else's. No minute's silence then.

Results

(For more information on biopsy results please visit www.prostatecanceruk.org)

5. Waiting

This chapter is called 'Waiting'. To be honest, every chapter could start with the word 'waiting'. Go and make a cup of tea. Settle down with some popcorn. We're going to be waiting. Waiting for results. Waiting for the next appointment. Waiting. Even my computer was doing it:
'Please wait' said the 'Windows' logo.

Trouble is I couldn't wait. Not forever. Time was not on my side.
I had to get a report out for a meeting. I checked the printer: 'Waiting in the queue'.
Then I was in the conference room with my print-out. A new day. A new slogan on the wall:
'Your lack of planning is somebody else's rush job.'

We were meeting to discuss making our best-selling product more portable. It would mean drastically reducing it in size. We were about to receive some guidance on how this would be achieved. Someone stood next to a large display screen with a magic wand. All was about to be revealed. Words appeared on the screen:
'Blue Sky Thinking.'
'Thinking out of the box.'
'Stretching the envelope.'
Loads more meaningless slogans. Feel free to add some from your own library. To quote one of my own we were:
'Pushing the boundaries of common sense'.
Despite it all, I was quite enthused. I always was. Once your enthusiasm was gone, cynicism filled the gap.

At home I looked at my prostate cancer booklet. The one with my own personal results written in it. I'd never read it properly. I'd get so far and see that bit of biro again and put it down. 'T3a' I could cope with, but the words 'breaking out' brought me out in a cold sweat.

It was shortly after receiving my results that I achieved a personal milestone. I'd made a 28-day catheter last -well, 28 days. It had gone full term. I was now ready for a grown-up catheter. The three month variety. I had no desire to see this catheter live a long and fulfilling life. No desire to get fully acquainted with it. If it wasn't out within a month I would be charging it rent. Following so closely after my diagnosis, if someone had told me this catheter would almost go full term as well, I would have been ever so slightly fed up. I phoned the district nurse and made an appointment. I gave her my address, a suitable time to call and yes, my catheter size. Didn't want another meeting with Vlad the Impaler.

June was off to do some shopping:
'Will you be alright on your own with the district nurse?'
'Of course' I lied.

I confess I was slightly anxious about this. There was so much scope for impropriety. My personal and private secretary had just gone to the shops. I was on my own. I was just the kind of person who, in a misguided effort to put everyone at ease, would come out with something totally crass and inappropriate. I had recently bumped into an ex work colleague who had left to have a baby. She still looked a little heavy almost twelve months on.
'Are further congratulations in order?'
'Er no. I just haven't quite..um..got back to where I was.'

Red faces all round. Another promising acquaintance ruined. My only saving grace was that I hadn't patted her on the stomach. Anyway, back to the present. I ran through my opening lines:
'Where do you want me?'
'Shall we go to my bedroom now?'
'Trousers and Pants?'

I was going to get undressed in front of a strange woman who was acting in a professional capacity. See what I mean? Even that sounds wrong. Part of me sensed the vulnerability of a woman meeting a stranger in unfamiliar surroundings. On that basis alone, I wanted the situation to be relaxed and friendly as soon as possible. Blimey. Why wasn't June here? She would find just the right words.
There was a knock on the door:
'Hello, -Mr Meredith?'
'Yes that's right, come on in.'

Ok so far. I had never started a conversation with a woman knowing that at some point she was **duty bound** to ask me to remove my underclothes and lie on a bed. This was an adolescent boy's dream. Should I mention the 'undress' word first? Or was the correct protocol to let her mention it first? I didn't want to get too far ahead of myself. I decided to be bashful. I'd let **her** mention it first. I wasn't **that** keen to get started.
I figured that if I said virtually nothing, I could avoid making a complete tit of myself.

'Nice day Mr Meredith.'
'Very nice. Yes. Very nice indeed. Yes'

Phew! I navigated that one ok. I was conscious that one of us was going to remove their clothes in front of the other at some point. I somehow guessed it would be me.
There was an awkward silence.
'They say it might rain later' I ventured.
'Yes. Coming in from the west' she replied getting some paperwork out.

We were in the front room. The 'undress' word would have to be uttered at some point. It was the elephant in the room. I had to navigate from the weather to the 'undress' word somehow. It was probably well beyond my technical capabilities. I needed to be tactful. There was a possibility of having my catheter changed in total silence with one of us red-faced with embarrassment.
I was wringing my hands together. Struggling to cope. There was another long pause. I felt duty bound to fill it with words:
'Shall we get started on the sofa or in my bedroom?'
Oh God. That sounded truly awful. I was skating on thin ice.
One more awkward silence like that and I could be in trouble.
'Upstairs would be best. I'll need some running water'.

I chose the spare room because the bathroom was across the landing. As I opened the door, I had a dreadful realisation that I hadn't checked the room for embarrassing objects. I guessed she must have seen it all by now. I wasn't worried about condoms. Not even a vibrator. Not even a sign saying 'Danger! Giant Penis'. Not a Daniel O'Donnel CD, not even some nail clippings. None of those things. I remembered the spare room was where I kept my Darth Vadar statue.
'Is here ok?'
'Yes. This will do.'

I started getting undressed. No good waiting for the starting gun. I was relieved to see she wasn't following my example. My trousers came down. Various objects appeared from out of her bag. I stretched out on the bed. My shirt covering my modesty. We were under way: I felt the coldness of an antiseptic wipe and made conversation -like you do.
'Been on any nice holidays this year?'
'Not really. I'm a bank nurse. I work in the UK in the summer - breathe in Mr Meredith -then spend the winter months in Spain in our villa. Now breathe out slowly.'
'That sounds like. Ohh!. Fu..fu..fun.'
'There. Half way stage. Everything OK?'
I nodded. Darth looked down benignly. He'd seen it all before on his inter-galactic travels.

I don't know what the neighbours thought. June goes out. A strange woman turns up, and there's groaning coming from the bedroom. I should have closed the window. Don't be fooled anyone. Having a catheter changed was far too drastic a measure simply to tempt an attractive woman into your bedroom. A few more groans from me and my three-month catheter was in. No smashed shop windows this time. No chimney pots falling into the street. I hoped my new high-volume water drinking technique would mean that blockages were going to be a thing of the past.
I thanked her and she was gone. I noticed the net curtain move in the house opposite. This catheter business was definitely getting easier. Not to the point where you might invite all your friends round for a catheter party. Just easier. I knew what to expect now.

As an apprentice I'd spent many a weekend with my fellow apprentices at Rhosilli beach on the Gower. We'd all made our canoes ourselves using a mould, and had spent many happy hours putting them to the test in the surf. Of course, with the passage of time, the stories had become more lurid with every telling: The biggest drinker medal, the largest turd medal (minus flies of course), and so on. You get the picture. I hadn't been there for such a long time. The beach was at least three miles long. I remembered a little white house half way along it -miles from anywhere. After a bit of time on Google I discovered that it had been a rectory. It was built for a rector who had to serve the parishes of Rhosilli and Llangennith, two villages that lay at opposite ends of the beach. I suppose it made sense to build it half way between them, but it meant this house stood completely alone. It was at least a mile from the nearest road and looked forlornly out to sea. I always wondered who lived there. Then I discovered it was owned by the National Trust. We were members. It was the most popular of all the holiday properties they rented out.

'Hey, look at this!'

June was at my shoulder.

'Where's the nearest hospital?'

I looked though the details.

'I don't think we need to worry about that -it's fully booked for at least twelve months. If we book the next available date, I won't have this anymore' I said, patting my lower leg.

June looked at the details.

'It's got four bedrooms. We ought to ask if anyone else wants to come. It seems a bit of a waste just to have the place to ourselves.'

'Ok I'll ask around.'

I booked it. I tried to look ahead. I imagined being sat at the window, looking out to sea. I would know my fate by then.

I was waiting for a bone scan which carried with it the possibility of grave consequences. It's a lonely place. Even with friends and family. Re-assurance is in short supply. As are listeners.

It occurred to me how difficult this would be if you were facing it alone.

I was having a 'low' day. A day when the endless waiting eroded my reserves of energy and confidence. I'd wait at the window, and helplessly watch the post-lady walk by without so much as a pause. I longed for her to stop, take a look in her bag, and return to our driveway excitedly waving my bone scan appointment. But then we all get low days, cancer or no cancer. My cure was usually to go for a long run, release those endorphins, but this wasn't possible in the company of Colin Catheter. Waiting is pain-free, but in my opinion it's easily the worst aspect of the whole thing.

I popped around to see my stepmother. She smoked twenty a day, but despite her best efforts she was as fit as a fiddle. I was round there to do her a favour -paint her garden fence. It was a bit difficult for her without some steps and she wasn't about to take any chances. She valued her independence. If I was good, I would get a pat on the back, a cup of tea and a biscuit. Then she would chat about my father. It was a regret of mine that I hadn't taken the time to really talk to him at the end. He went so suddenly. We didn't notice that each time he bounced back from a blood transfusion, he didn't bounce back quite so far. I had the usual regrets about not really talking to him. At least this way I could talk to someone who really knew him.

Sometimes you have to tell someone how you really feel about them while they are still alive, but that was easier said than done.

Especially for me for some reason. My excuse was that I didn't want him to think I was giving up on him. Like I say -it was an excuse.
They had played bowls together. Her display cabinet was testament to their skill. I used to jokingly call it the 'trophy cabinet'. When my first marriage had ended, they gave me somewhere to live. It had been quite a distressing time and I needed a bit of emotional support. Well more than a bit if I'm honest. Their spare room was my lifeboat. They would come in from bowls and share a smoke. Analysing every shot. What they could have done better. They were a team. She had no children of her own and when she married my father, we were part of his baggage train.

June and I were also a team. June was happy to follow my lead while I navigated a path through the great issues of the day. Our position on Brexit. Our joint view on the expansion of NATO into the Baltic States. Whether the Elgin marbles should be returned to Greece. How to react to the new President of the United States.
In return June looked after life's minutia: Birthdays, Christmas Day, where we went on holiday, the choice of family car and what house we lived in. Everyday stuff.

My stepmother was always interested in what I was getting up to. What was going on in my life. She knew about my diagnosis. She had first-hand experience of what might lie ahead, but spared me the details. She knew better than to talk about that. She nursed my father during the last two years of his life. She had been so dependable. So reliable. His medication was constantly changing and each time she would read the small print on the labels. On several occasions she'd go back to the doctor and complain that drug X couldn't be taken with drug Y. She was with him right to the end. She shouldered the burden while we just got on with our lives.

I was painting her garden fence. Lost in my thoughts.
'Hey Sunshine, -you missed a bit!'
I turned around. She stood there smiling. Leaning against the wall. Cigarette in hand.
'Sorry. I was miles away.'
'Hmm. I suppose I shouldn't be surprised.'
'Anyway, you're relieved of your duties for a minute, the kettle's just boiled.'

She had done a wonderful job looking after my father, and after his funeral I promised myself that I would look after her on his behalf. I hoped that when the time came, I would be strong enough to do for her what she had done for him. Of course, I had never shared this thought with her, but something told me I didn't need to. She was perceptive. As sharp as a pin. I suspected she might already know. I was executor of her will and had been granted power of attorney. She had put her faith in me. While she went off to fetch the chocolate biscuits, it struck me that maybe I wouldn't get the chance to carry out what I'd promised.

I could go weeks without speaking to her. She didn't want to be a burden. She only asked me for help when she really couldn't manage by herself. She recently had a leak in the roof of her bungalow. It was bad enough to cause a part of the ceiling to fall onto the floor. She didn't panic. Just phoned up a few builders and got some quotes. By the time I knew about it she'd got the quotes in and just wanted me to confirm that the sums of money were reasonable. She was easy to talk to. Knew when to say something and when to keep quiet.

I'd been suffering from a bad back. I knew that a back problem had prompted my father to get help. They'd discovered bone cancer in his lower back and pelvis. The cancer had started in the prostate and had spread to surrounding areas. I wasn't concerned enough to share my back problem with my stepmother. I was pretty sure my bad back was caused by a parachute jump I did with my apprentice friends many years ago. It was the debt I paid for being reckless. When I shared this information with my work colleagues, some wag joked that I'd done in at Arnhem in World War Two. Anyway, I digress. My bad back came and went. Despite it all, I couldn't be entirely sure, but worrying about it wasn't going to help me now. It was just a question of waiting.

I sat there with my cup of tea. I watched the milk make a spiral, lost in my thoughts.
She brought me back to the present:
'Earth to moon. Earth to Moon. Are you receiving us?'
'Ha! Sorry. Miles away again.'
'How are you anyway?'
'I'm ok. Thanks for asking. I suppose I shouldn't be surprised. They say that if your father has had prostate cancer you are at greater risk.'
She sighed:
'I know but **three generations!**'
'Sorry?'
She gave me a curious look.
'Your grandfather, your dad's dad. Didn't you know?'
'Seriously?'
'Sorry David. I thought you knew.' Her voice tailed away 'I wouldn't have said...'
I shook my head:

'Don't worry. It's not your fault. I knew he died of cancer..I just didn't know it was prostate cancer.'

I thought back to that first urinary tract infection. The warning sign that had been missed. It's no good blaming anyone. Not now. I was probably partially to blame. Always so keen to escape the clutches of the medical profession. Never wanting to ask questions. She knew better than to offer assurances. Much better. She moved the discussion on.
'Any news on the bone scan?'
'It's been three weeks since my diagnosis. Still no news.'
I told her about my conversation with Kate, my assigned nurse.
'I told her that it's not contained within the prostate -that it's breaking out. You'd think that would make it a priority'.
'It must be difficult.'
'To be honest it's not too bad. It's just a cautionary scan. It's the time it takes. It'll be ok.'
'Another cup of tea?'
'Any more jobs?'
'No. You've finished early for the day.'
'Oh, that's good. I'll get the scrabble out. My luck is about to change. You're in for a hammering!'
After the game I mentioned the cottage, but she was going to be away on a bowls tour and wouldn't be able to make it.
I felt better. Not only for being able to unburden myself, but the act of helping someone else -the *giving* of my time, seemed to lift my mood. Helped me forget my troubles. There was probably some profound philosophical reason for this -not that I was going to discover what it was.

With the current uncertainty over my future, even the most innocuous questions took on a whole new meaning. There was a collective groan around the office. We had all just received an e-mail informing us that our performance appraisals were imminent. In due course a date appeared in our calendar.

'Blimey Dave! You got that report done pretty quick!' said a colleague.

'Well my appraisal is due. I had to turn on the afterburners!'

We laughed. It was a joke. You couldn't get away with 'making an effort' just once a year.

In a previous work environment in a different age, I knew someone who regularly went out and got his hair cut in company time. His manager hauled him into his office and demanded to know how he could justify such a thing:

'Well it grows in company time! I might as well get it cut in company time!'

We were set objectives and targets. These flowed down from the highest level —our managing director. They were passed quickly down the food chain like a hot potato. They quickly reached the lower levels. They usually consisted of something profound like 'Make more money'. The appraisal form usually consisted of 'what' and 'why' questions, which were designed to provoke a thoughtful response. My problem was the same for anyone my age: I had a promising career behind me. The most troublesome question as you got older was the one linked to your future career. The format of the question changed from time to time. The question this time was framed in this manner:

'Where do you see yourself in five years time?'

As you approached retirement this question was not taken too seriously, but it did make me stop and contemplate my future. My manager gave me a tight smile and moved on to the next question.

I was watching the post-lady again. I'd been showing far more interest in her than was good for my relationship. She turned into our drive. Was that a hint of a smile?
At last!
I have a date for my bone scan, the 24th January. I expected every church bell in the country to peal with joy. Signal beacons to be lit on every hill. A few days later I was off to the hospital.
I was early. I hadn't read the letter properly. Only after I arrived, did I discover I wasn't due for another hour. The first clue to my timekeeping error was when I touched the 'self-register' screen to find it had no record of me. 'You can only register your arrival within 30 minutes of your appointment' it told me. I had no choice but to go to the girl at the desk. She looked at her screen.
'You're a bit early Mr Meredith'
'I couldn't wait to get here.'
'Well I've registered your arrival now. Please take a seat.'

After a short wait, a radioactive tracer was injected into my vein. An even longer wait ensued while the tracer reached every part of my body. I was feeling pretty relaxed –my treatment was moving forwards. Apart from slight claustrophobia, I didn't have a problem with scans. There was no prodding involved.
Then I lay on a bed and headed off into a tunnel. The nicest aspect of this scan, especially if you are unfortunate enough to suffer from claustrophobia, was that your choice of music could be played while you lay in the confines of the scanning machine. It helped you relax. I really made the most of this. I chose:

'First cut is the deepest' -Cat Stevens.
'Bend me shape me' – Amen Corner (ideal for plastic surgery operations).
'Don't go breaking my heart' –Kiki Dee and Elton John.
I avoided anything by the Grateful Dead, and 'I just died in your arms tonight' by the Cutting Crew was a definite no-no.

Eventually, when they'd had enough of my weird playlist, they sent me home.
I'm kidding you here. I didn't have **complete** freedom of choice. That would have been unfair on the staff. I chose Classic FM.

'How did it go?' asked June as I came through the door.
'It was ok. I didn't feel anything. I've got to stay away from babies and pregnant women for 24 hours'
'When will you get the results?'
'They're going to phone me in an hour.'
'What?'
'I'm joking. They weren't able to tell me.'

I young person might radiate health. I was actually radiating. I was cycling to play skittles tonight. Maybe I wouldn't need any lights. Of course, now the scan had taken place, my anxiety switched to the results. I'd had a CT scan, an MRI scan, an Ultrasound scan and now a Bone Scan. June gave voice to my feelings:
'I keep thinking that they missed an opportunity when you had that first UTI. I hope it's not too late.'

I smiled as best I could. The waiting would soon be over. Soon I would know my fate. I did a bit more work on the doll's house. I began to look at it in a different way. My daughter's house was her pride and joy. When my son-in-law got interested in moving home, she told him the only way she would ever leave the house was if they carried her out in a coffin. I hoped she would appreciate my hard work. My uncertain future meant I was now in 'legacy' mode.

I paused by the front door. Took a breath. Put my smile on. Another day at work. Another day without news. It was almost a week since my bone scan and almost **three months** since my biopsy. Someone in the hospital must already know my fate. Maybe I was just sat in an electronic 'in tray' while more urgent results were waved through.

I was a fire warden. It was time to test the fire alarms. There was a switch panel in the lobby which enabled you to test the alarm without alerting the fire brigade. It was a two-man job. One person activated the little 'break glass' alarm activator, and the other stood by the switch panel ready to silence the alarm.
The system was maintained by an outside company, and I remembered when it was first installed. Immediately after its first service we experienced a problem. We had just tested the alarm successfully and had returned to our desks.
We didn't pay much attention to the distant sound of a fire engine. It was just another fire engine on a call. As soon as you became aware of the siren it usually faded into the distance. This one was more persistent though. It gradually got louder. The engine was on our industrial estate somewhere and people looked up from their desks. Some of us made our way to the windows to see which building it was heading for. We could see it now. It turned into our road making quite a lot of noise. We looked up and down the road but couldn't see any smoke. Then my heart sank. As more and more

people came to the windows, I saw it turn into our car park. There was a screech of brakes.

Men jumped out -ready to perform heroics.

Vaughan, the other fire warden, followed me down to the lobby. We were both a bit red-faced. He began to laugh and sensed his opportunity. As I rushed out of the door, he bolted into a broom cupboard. Suddenly, I was alone on the tarmac. Heads poked out of distant windows. They saw a red-faced chap begin a prolonged episode of bowing and scraping. The chief officer was pretty good natured about it -at least to my face. They piled back onto the engine as I walked backwards into our building with even more deference. The other fire warden appeared at my side as we made our way back into the office. He was in fits of giggles:

'The look on your face Dave when all those hoses came out!'

Well I suppose it was quite funny. These things always are after the event, especially if someone else has taken the flak.

'We're a team aren't we Vaughan? Just thought I'd check!'

From that point on everyone knew who I was. I was the warden who got the fire engine out.

In my defence I was the only one with actual fire-fighting experience. Ok it was only a smouldering cigarette, but it was still **technically** a fire. Material had been combusting **and** I had dealt with it unaided. Unaided, except for a cup of water that is.

As I rose from my seat to test the alarm, there were the familiar calls from some of my colleagues to rush to the windows and watch the fire engine. Unless you were Albert Einstein, you could do some outstanding work, but only your disasters were ever remembered until the end of time. You were defined by them and were never allowed to forget them.

It was no good reminding them it had been the fault of the company who serviced the system.
I tried a different tack:
'I am the best fire warden in the building -no one has ever caught fire on my watch.'
Oh well. Another fire alarm test completed.
Another day closer to my scan result.

The doll's house was going well. The conservatory was full of cavity walls made out of mdf, sash windows and panelled doors. Building work had spread beyond the conservatory. This wasn't a situation that June would normally be happy with, but I was being indulged. I'd got into the habit of going into work slightly late so I could see the post being delivered. Six days had elapsed since the bone scan. Four weeks had elapsed since my diagnosis. I'd sourced bag-loads of little cardboard squares for the roof tiles. The walls were going up. Floors were sliding into grooves. It was looking impressive even though I say so myself. The house must have been a metre square. June was full of encouragement:
'Christ, they must have built the real thing quicker than the time you've spent on this.'
I did think about changing my name to 'Howmuch Meredith' around this time, because after every trip to Hobbycraft that's how I would be greeted as I came in through the door.
It was filling my spare hours. Stopping both of us from dwelling on things. Like the future. Like how we would manage. How we would tell people. It stopped me thinking about how time was drifting by.

'Slow moving' Kate had said. 'Slow moving' was my mantra. Fingers crossed. June punched a hole in my thoughts:
'One slight problem.'

'What's that? I asked fitting a little fireplace.
'How are you going to get it out of the house?'
I stepped back, looked around. She was right. The French windows led into the back garden but then there was insufficient space down the sides of the house to enable the doll's house to reach the driveway and be loaded into a van. Going forwards, neither the hallway nor the front door would be wide enough to cope with it.
'Ha Ha!'
She folded her arms. Her right foot tapped the ground. She gave a look of triumph. I had to think of something. Couldn't let her win. She pointed a finger at me:
'Gotcha!'
'No you haven't!' I replied airily. 'I'm going out of the French windows, and down to the bottom of the garden.'
'What good is that?'
'Well, I'll take a fence panel out, and continue on past the house beyond and down his drive to reach the next road along.'
'Huh! We don't even know their names or where they live!'
'Not yet we don't!'

The Dolls House was a welcome distraction. It stopped me dwelling on my uncertain future. In writing this book I have tried to be light-hearted. Tried to be positive. However, if you find yourself in this situation, your thoughts will take you to some dark places. I found myself carefully looking at everyday things. Really looking. Using my senses. The shape and form of a daffodil. The smell of a hyacinth. The call of a blackbird. I'd spent the whole of my life in such a restless way. Getting anxious if I couldn't fill a spare half-hour. Now I want to get off the merry-go-round and watch for a while.

I was reminded of a poem by William Henry Davies. It summed up my mood during these trying times:

What is this life if, full of care,
We have no time to stand and stare
No time to stand beneath the boughs
And stare as long as sheep or cows.
No time to see, when woods we pass,
Where squirrels hide their nuts in grass
No time to see, in broad daylight,
Streams full of stars, like skies at night.
No time to turn at Beauty's glance,
And watch her feet, how they can dance.
No time to wait till her mouth can
Enrich that smile her eyes began.
A poor life this if, full of care,
We have no time to stand and stare.

If it was bad news, I started to consider how best to use the time I had left. For some it would be fancy holidays in faraway places. For others, quality time with family. Maybe meaningful conversation. Certainly not a supermarket shop or mowing the lawn. Although I couldn't afford to go on some uproariously indulgent world tour, I could at least pay someone else to do my chores. I looked at an old photo of my christening. Mum didn't go through the pain of childbirth, and endure all those sleepless nights, just so I could waste my time painting the spare room. I could tell by the way she looked down at my cherubic little face, that she had a more meaningful and fulfilling destiny in mind. Trouble is, neither of us ever found out what that was. Now was the time to seek and find.

To ponder meaning and destiny. Those words were coming into sharper focus now.

I could say I have good days and bad days, but I don't. In fact, I feel perfectly fine, every day. There's no pain. No lumps for me to fret over. Only the catheter reminds me that there's a problem somewhere.

I had a problem if the news was bad. At sixty-two, I still needed to earn a living. My savings wouldn't see me through. My company provided life insurance. In order for June to benefit, would I technically still have to be an employee when the end came? What were the terms and conditions relating to death in service? Maybe I could switch to part time -gradually reducing my hours as things got worse.

The need to earn money had been a driving imperative from quite a young age and now, even with this threat hanging over me, it couldn't be ignored. These were the questions that might have to be faced. Anyway, enough of this. You can get depressed by yourself. You don't need me for that.

I'm sleeping well. There's no getting up for the loo in the middle of the night to disturb you. The catheter takes care of that. I wouldn't risk five pints of lager before going to bed though. Even the bed bag won't be able to cope with that kind of volume. No doubt your body would find some way of waking you up to deal with the problem. Your carefree dream might morph into one where you're convinced you've got urine trickling out of your ears. Not everyone sleeps well though. I've been told I have a slight snoring issue. Not all the time you understand -only when I'm breathing. Apparently, there's a race to be the first person to fall asleep. Of course, I'm totally unaware of any competition, and in this relaxed state my snoring inevitable starts about three breaths in. June can't compete.

Now, with the benefit of the catheter, I don't disturb her sleep further with visits to the loo.

She did buy a few packets of ear plugs once, but I kept blowing them out of my mouth.

I wake up. I feel relaxed. Almost carefree. The sun is streaming in through the windows. Thanks to the catheter, I've slept right through the night.

Unbeknown to me, something has been waiting patiently for me to wake from my slumber. It sits on my bedside table. It's vigilant, knowing and grimly determined. It's waiting to pounce:

It's the 'C' word.

As soon as I wake up, it leaps into my head and dominates my every conscious thought. It won't leave me alone until I go back to sleep that evening. Even then it might not leave me be. It's my constant companion -as well as the catheter of course. I look at my bed bag. Pretty full, which is good. Catheter working ok. A positive thought.

I get up. Pick up my bed bag and head to the bathroom to empty it. I aim for the side of the toilet bowl. I don't want to make it sound like I'm running a bath. How wonderful.

Now I switch over to the leg-bag for the day ahead. I'm not ignoring my situation. Not burying my head in the sand. The leg-bag makes sure of that. I'm wondering if it would help to talk to someone about it. But who? Maybe there's a Facebook group page for catheter wearers. It would be a place of high membership turnover and sad emojis.

Deep down I know the bone scan is just a precaution. They don't want to waste money on a major operation if the cancer has already spread elsewhere. I know that the odds are that it will be fine. It's just the time that's ticking by. I'm busy at work and the doll's house keeps me busy at home, so I'm managing to keep it out of my thoughts. Most of the time. I have to. I wouldn't be able to concentrate on anything otherwise. Only a visit to the loo reminds me that my plumbing system is currently undergoing a rethink. Then I look at the calendar. I've got through another week. Another week without progress.

I've spoken to the H.R. department. They promise to be supportive whatever the outcome. My manager knows. I just don't know who else does. I presume hardly anyone. Don't be silly now, plenty of people know. It's just not spoken about. At least not in front of me. It was time for work. No post. Another day without news

I waved my security card at the door. An argument raged in my head. To be honest, it was more like a shouting match:
'Breaking out'.
'Slow moving'.
'Breaking out' and so on. Fortunately, I was able to stay positive most of the time and 'slow moving' was able to prevail. I put my 'face' on.

With retirement advancing over the horizon people at work would often take the mickey. With sexism and racism off the menu, ageism is all they have left poor things. Of course, you have to make light of it:
'At my age I don't buy green bananas anymore' I joked.
'Or long-life batteries!' quipped some wag.

If they didn't know, I could hardly expect them to behave any differently. Actually, it seemed better that they didn't know. Work became a sanctuary where I could enjoy my usual banter with my colleagues without having to think about cancer. This was my approach –it wouldn't suit everyone. Be as public or as private as you want with your diagnosis, but bear in mind you'll need an area of your life where you can be free to forget about cancer for a while.

We had a number of first-aiders in the building. No point in involving them in my prognosis - it was well beyond the scope of their experience. I didn't want some over-enthusiastic first-aider coming up to me carrying a de-fibrillator, or even worse, approaching me with pouted lips ready to administer the kiss of life. I knew some of our first-aiders well. The improvement they would be able to effect on my well-being would be marginal at best.

I'd been a first-aider once, one with legendary healing powers. A women had once fainted in the summer heat, only to miraculously revive once she was aware that I was on my way to administer mouth to mouth resuscitation.

As the morning progressed, I began to notice slightly more weight on the one leg as I walked about. I don't even need to look. I'm an expert. I need to empty my leg-bag:
'If anyone asks' I shouted to my tormentors, 'I'm just popping up to HR to update my date of birth!'
I prop a leg on the toilet seat, roll my trouser leg up, and open the tap on my leg-bag. The toilet has a motion sensitive light and I have to wave an arm to keep it on. Oh joy. Then I'm good to go. Wash my hands. Roll my trouser-leg back down. One last check before I

exit the loo: make sure the drain tube isn't showing below my trouser hem. Don't get careless. Always check. If you get the tell-tale downward look from a colleague, the embarrassment will be so acute, you won't be able to get the 'prosthetic leg, hydraulic pipe' excuse out quick enough.

And for God's sake remember to close the tap, otherwise the feeling of 'I've been here before' won't just be a philosophical question -you'll be able to see the tell-tale drips on the carpet.

This is just supposition you understand -I'm not speaking from experience here.

I returned to the office.

My phone was ringing. Outside call. I hurried to my desk. The phone displayed the telephone number of the incoming call. I snatched it up to my ear:

'June?'

6. Discussing the options

'Dave? I've just had a phone call from Kate. Your nurse.'
She sounded emotional. Time slowed to a stop. I analysed every inflexion in her voice. Every tone of every vowel. The whole office seemed to pause. People stopped in mid-stride.
'Your Bone scan is all good.'

'Dave? Are you there?'

'Dave?'
I slumped in my chair. Head in hands. The phone lay on the desk.
'Say something!' it squeaked.
'Yes. I...I'm fine.'
My eyes flicked around the local vicinity. Everyone seemed absorbed in their work. Nevertheless, it wasn't the best place for a private phone call.
I heard a sniff on the end of the line. Her voice seemed to break:
'She phoned me a few minutes ago. I've got Anne with me.'
'We've both been in tears here.'
I was glad June was doing the talking. Somebody had to.

You can never tell how much pressure you're under until it's suddenly taken away. You've been managing it for so long. When it's replaced by good news it's like an emotional dam giving way. Like you've been held under water and been allowed to come up for air.
I thought of my Father. My grandfather. They never experienced this. This gift of good news.
'Thanks for letting me know.'

Discussing the options

'Ok I'll see you later. You alright?'
'I am now. See you soon.'
I put the phone down.
I stood up. Didn't know what to do with myself.
'You alright Dave?'
It was Mark. My line-manager. He knows my situation. I take a breath:
'My bone scan is all good.'
Even as the words come out, I feel I'm losing my composure.
'I'm good to go on the Op.'
He smiles. I rub my forehead, shield my eyes.
'I'll be back in a moment.'
Phew. I'm sat in the disabled loo. My refuge. I close my eyes. A weight has been lifted. I couldn't laugh. Couldn't cry either. There was just an overwhelming feeling of relief. I sat there. Remained still. Then the light went out.

I was already aware that at my local hospital, a prostatectomy was performed using the very latest 'Da Vinci Robotic System'. Mr Google was providing me with images. I'd wanted to look at this for such a long time but I didn't want to tempt fate. Now I was getting excited about it in the same way a normal person might over the purchase of a new car. I sent a picture of it to my inner circle. I would guess if you're reading this book you may already have a clear vision of what this system looks like. For those that don't, think car production lines and those robotic arms that reach into the body of the car to make the little welds that join it all together. Now substitute some poor bloke for the car. Over to one side a surgeon operates the whole thing remotely from a computer screen.

Discussing the options

The replies came thick and fast.

They thought I was making the whole thing up. That I had actually photoshopped the car out and put a man in its place. They would not be convinced until they had googled it for themselves. Part of me was very humbled by the fact that I was going to be dealt with by this state-of-the-art piece of technology. I replied to the doubters:

'They're operating on 'moi'. They're hardly going to use a scalpel, are they?'

Nothing could have spoilt my mood that day. Not even one of the dreaded e-mails from the man at the top, which just appeared in my in-box.

We were an American-owned company and the 'man-at-the-top' was currently someone called 'Carson' living in Michigan. These communications were full of meaningless corporate jargon, and were opened and immediately forgotten about. However, the latest opus dealt with our merger with a rival company and its impact on inter-planetary trading. I sat back in wonderment. This was an exceptionally fine specimen of corporate communication, and needed to be shared with an undeserving world:

'This merger creates synergies driving further engagement with key stakeholders to deliver best-in-class mission-critical solutions across all domains in order to become the non-traditional sixth prime. This merger synthesises the strategic rationale required to architect the new company so that in meeting our commitments we open the strategic door to strengthen our international footprint and competitive discriminators against the competition. We're aligning our strategy, investment resources and partners to execute inside our competitor's timelines and migrating to the next

Discussing the options

step in our strategic cadence as we work towards becoming a world leader in the supply of sandy coloured boxes.'

Of course, to maintain the thrust and tempo of the narrative, punctuation is kept to a minimum or dispensed with altogether. For health and safety reason, don't attempt to say this at home – you may expire due to lack of oxygen.
In my euphoric state, I almost rose from my seat, looked to the heavens with a fist held aloft and shouted:
'Carson, I'm right behind you boy!'

Monday. A letter dropped onto the mat. A pre-operation appointment with my surgeon. Things were moving forward. I was feeling happier than I had in ages. If I could bottle this feeling, I'd be a rich man.
It was a 'dressing down' day at work. No, not a day where you might get a telling off. That could happen at any time. No, it was a charity day where in turn for a donation, you could wear pretty much what you liked. It was a nice change from the usual shirt and tie. Judging by the way some of my colleagues dressed, they must be donating every day. We were collecting for 'Children in Need'. June scrutinised my attire. Years ago, when we both worked at the same company, I'd rushed out of the house with two different coloured shoes on, only for her to send me home at lunchtime once she'd been alerted by her secretarial colleagues.

'You're not wearing that to work -it's truly ancient.'
'It's a charity t-shirt! It'll be fine. I'm not customer facing. This is a collector's item.'
'So are most of your clothes!'
I responded with my usual mantra:

'I go without, so you don't have to.'
'Well I'm going to clear your wardrobe. It's about time I brought you into the twenty-first century.'

'Blast!'
A meeting appointment popped up in my outlook calendar. A meeting with a Human Resources (HR) lady to discuss my situation, and I really wasn't very well dressed. The reminder had occurred too late. The meeting had been arranged to manage the prolonged absence from work demanded by my operation.
Another meeting room, another slogan:
'It takes twenty years to build a reputation, and five minutes to ruin it.'
Blimey – I don't know whether I even got started on that one. Whatever remained of my reputation was about to be lost, once she clapped eyes on my t-shirt.
Our HR lady swept into the room. I needn't have worried. I was sat opposite an HR professional, clothed from top to bottom in a full length yellow 'Children in Need' outfit. My 'Live Aid' t-shirt paled in comparison. She assured me that everything was taken care of, and that 'Pudsey' would ensure that the company's monthly donation would continue without any problem.

When I got back to the office, there was a phone call.
'Dave, Goods Inwards here. We've got a parcel for you.'
This was highly unusual. I was straight down there.
He reached up to a shelf. There were parcels and deliveries from all our usual suppliers. Things like electronic components, cables and machined housings. He pushed a 'Thorntons' package towards me: 'You've obviously made an impression with someone Dave!'

Discussing the options

I was puzzled -maybe it was SAGA's latest introductory offer. Most of the introductory offers coming my way these days were do-it-yourself wills or funeral plans. I improvised:
'Oh er..It's for a customer'.
He tapped the side of his nose:
'Your secret's safe with me Dave!'

I was back at my desk. I had to open it. I couldn't take it home. Well, not until I'd found out who it was from. Maybe it was from a secret admirer. I was hopeless at reading the signs. A woman would have to walk up to me and plant a smacker straight on the lips -with tongues, and I'd still think she was trying to give me the kiss of life. Blimey, she'd better be quick. I was heading into platonic relationship territory. Maybe it was from a woman who wanted me for my mind and personality. Even my fertile imagination couldn't stretch that far. Off came the wrapper. A box of 'Thorntons' finest with a message card.
It was from my daughter.

What a wonderful thought. Sent to my place of work as well. I confess: I wiped away a tear. If you know someone with cancer, or any illness for that matter, do not underestimate the power of thoughtfulness. It could be a child's hand-drawn card or a homemade cake. It doesn't matter. Don't let that tough exterior fool you. We men all have our weak spots, and it isn't too hard to find them. I wanted to tell everybody what a lovely surprise it had been, but then I'd have to come up with a reason for it. I tucked them under my desk and tried to compose myself. I floated on a cloud for the rest of the day. I told everyone that June had increased my medication.

Discussing the options

Things were moving rapidly now. 'Rapid' being a relative term. I now had an appointment with someone quite high up the medical food chain: My surgeon. I'd never met a real one – only seen them on the telly. It was just a talk. I didn't have to turn up with a full bladder and I was assured that no prodding was involved.

'Come on in Mr Meredith'. It was Kate -my assigned nurse
'Mr Hopton will be along in a moment'. I made small talk, trying to avoid my default response which by now was to remove my trousers.
'Weather's been nice?'
She almost twitched with energy, like there were a million things she really ought to be doing. This was probably the longest pause she'd enjoyed all week.
Then a door opened. There was a rush of air. It ruffled Kate's fringe. A blurr in front of me reached out a hand:
'Ah Mr Meredith -I'm Paul -your surgeon.'
Pieces of A4 fluttered down onto the table.
A quick hand-shake and he was rotating in his chair. I don't think his bottom was **actually** in contact with the seat of the chair. He seemed to hover a few inches above it, like he was levitating.
He pressed a button. A screen flickered into life:
'Your bone scan looks fine.'
A grey outline appeared with darker elements. It was ghostly -like it was no longer alive. My eyes danced over the image. It was the first time I had seen my own skeleton. I usually associated such images with an archaeological dig. With people who were no longer with us. It was unnerving.
Despite claims to the contrary, a back bone was indeed present.
I would have recoiled in my chair had there been enough time.

Discussing the options

I suddenly recalled something Spock had said to Captain James T Kirk:
'It's life Jim -but not as we know it.'
The image faded away.

'Your lymph nodes are all good, so we can now look forward to preparing for the operation. Your cancer is T3a which means it's breaking out of the capsule.'
Those words filled me with dread. He's talking about a biopsy that occurred over three months ago. Has it stayed put? It could be backpacking around the world by now. 'Slow moving' Kate had assured me.
'We need positive margins around the prostate. This means that in order to be safe we need to take away tissue beyond the prostate in the region where it's breaking out. Have you heard of nerve sparing?'
I nodded. Wonder-weapon was well aware of this. Two bundles of nerves each side of the prostate which were responsible for erections. Sparing one bundle meant it was possible for erections to return. The loss of both bundles made it very unlikely.

'Unfortunately, we will have to remove the nerves on one side of the prostate in order to be safe. I'm hoping to spare the nerves on the other side.'

Wonder-weapon cheered up for the first time since I overruled him and decided to have my prostate out. He had promised me that he would do the best he could with just the one bundle. We were best buddies again.

Discussing the options

'After removal of the prostate I will anastomose – join -the urethra to the neck of the bladder. You will be fitted with a catheter after the operation to allow the bladder to drain while the healing process takes place. It's important that you look after this catheter. Come straight into A&E if there is *any* sign of blockage.'

I was a qualified catheter carer. Me and my latest catheter had been intimate for six weeks now. I had forged a long-term relationship with this one. We were drinking partners. I pledged to drink at least three litres of water a day, and in return he promised to stay blockage-free. I knew what to do. It was simple. Follow the advice. Drink a-b-s-o-l-u-t-e-l-y loads.
The surgeon was in full flow. He would have to stop and inhale at some point. The air crackled with tension:

'As you are aware, we have the latest equipment here. Your Laparoscopic Prostatectomy will be performed with the assistance of the Da Vinci Robotic system. Recovery is quicker with this system. Any questions Mr Meredith?'

He finally stopped for breath. He almost quivered with restless energy like the next guy should have been in an hour ago. I suspected there weren't going to be any thoughtful silences. No leaning back in the chair for a moment's reflection while you both light up a cigar.
My chance to speak. To ask. The tempo of the meeting had been so fast that I felt compelled to make every word, every syllable count. I had to be succinct. To the point. Like the words were coming out of a machine gun. It was like a brief audience with the Dalai Lama where you have five seconds to ask something profound like: 'what was the meaning of life?'

Discussing the options

I wanted to be helpful. Share the burden:
'Do I need to shave myself? '
'No, we go in further up. There will be five incisions across the stomach, approximately level with your belly button. There will also be a drain hole.'
Belly button? That was at the very least 300mm away from my prostate. I was incredulous. Were they taking the scenic route? What Sat-Nav were they using? They needed to catch it unawares, not give it chance to take hostages or plead for clemency.
A-ha! Got it. Tactical diversion. Make it look as if you were heading for some other major organ, and then swing round and catch it by surprise. Master-stroke.

'We'll try and get that in-dwelling catheter removed and get you self-catheterising. It will enable you to live a much more normal life.'
I felt wonder-weapon nod in approval. Like someone down there already knew the implications. He knew what the words 'normal life' meant. No permanent in-dwelling catheter. He would be free to explore once again. One final fling.
'Kate, can you make the arrangements? You will receive a letter shortly Mr Meredith with an appointment for the operation. Well, if that's everything….'.

I was with my dentist, Imogen. She stood there rubbing her hands together in glee:
'Ah! Meesta Meredith. Vee have a filling for you today!'
I remembered when she first became my dentist. I confessed my dislike of the drill and she told me with a mischievous smile:
'That zee bit I like best!'

Discussing the options

Well I had to laugh, and in doing so I found myself relaxing into the chair.

'Well I'm glad someone's going to enjoy it.' I smiled.

'Relax Mr Meredith. Everything vill be fine.'

Everything really did turn out fine. She was the best dentist I ever had. I never felt anything, and never spent long in the chair.

She had a way of putting you at ease. She made me feel like the most important patient at the practice. I probably exaggerate: she made my **molars** feel like they were the most important things at the practice. I suppose I should be consoled by the knowledge that my discomfort was providing enjoyment for someone else.

'Any medications? Hospital visits?'

Suddenly I had to stop and think. I'd always been able to answer 'No'.

'Well -I've had some hospital visits. I'm about to go in for a prostatectomy.'

'Hmmm'

She looked thoughtful.

'You've had some scans? Barium injections?'

I nodded.

'OK. Take a seat and make yourself comfortable.'

I popped my finger inside my mouth and put my smile in a dish. There were still plenty of other targets for the high speed drill however.

She leant over me, her piercing blue eyes focussed on the task in hand. Then a quick whine of the drill. I'm sure she was smiling behind the mask. I had her undivided attention. I wouldn't ordinarily get this much attention from a woman. I'd always been 'left unattended' as far as the opposite sex were concerned.

Afterwards she spoke to me about gums and flossing. She gave me her serious look:

Discussing the options

'You must try and take more care of your gums.'

'Yes. I'll give it a go.'

While I was in the surgery, I meant every word. In that moment there was nothing I wanted more than to turn up six months later and get a pat on the back. A big smile. I had always been such a nervous patient but with Imogen I found it possible to relax for the very first time.

I knew that once I was out of the surgery my good intentions would just drift away on the breeze. I'd tried flossing and just couldn't do it. Even my electric toothbrush just got thrown in a drawer. I couldn't stick with that either. I just plugged away with my toothbrush, twice a day.

I got up. Put my smile back in. Thanked them and headed towards the door.

'Meesta Meredith?' she said, as I pulled the door open.

I turned towards her. She looked stern.

Her eyes met mine and she raised her index finger:

'Look after yourself.'

7. The Catheter Years -Part 2

After three months with an in-dwelling catheter, I could honestly say that I had experienced everything it had to offer. My reward was to be given the option of self-catheterising. Whatever that might be. They made it sound like progress. I was on board. So was my bestie down below.

Self-catheterising was practised with a 'single use' catheter. When the bladder needed emptying, the catheter would be inserted, pushed up through the prostate and into the bladder to allow it to drain. Then it was disposed of. Every time you needed to empty your bladder, the process would be repeated with a new catheter. I'd had an in-dwelling catheter fitted and removed four times. The first two had been removed due to blockage. The third was replaced because it was only a 28-day catheter. Each time there had been various levels of discomfort. I supposed I was now going to experience this amount of discomfort on a daily basis. I considered abandoning the idea but I'd been assured that it was for my benefit.

I was an 'old hand' in the catheter game and wonder-weapon had already made representations -it wasn't just my decision you understand. He would be off the leash.

Constrained by an in-dwelling catheter, wonder-weapon could do no more than creep uselessly down my leg. Well, my upper thigh if I'm honest. Ok. Ok. I confess:

My lower pelvis.

But self-catheterising meant that wonder-weapon was free to roam. He was my bestie. I had to take his feelings into account. There was one other obvious benefit: it couldn't get blocked.

Another hospital appointment. I was taken into a private room. Before I could self-catheterise, my 3-month indwelling catheter had to be removed. Like me it was coming to the end of its useful life. I would be glad to see it go, even though I wasn't sure what was going to replace it. I wasn't going to keep it as a momento. It was the same nurse that had removed it when I had my bad blockage. I wondered whether, as she recognised my face, a parallel picture of my nether regions popped up alongside. This was now pretty much a routine procedure for me. Progress indeed.

Trousers down. Catheter out. Trousers up. Dignity restored. I then had to drink some water until my bladder was comfortably full.

Then I was shown into the office of a nurse practitioner. I was invited to sit at her desk. She had an enlarged model of the most important part of a man's body. At least I think it was enlarged. I tried to avoid comparisons. I wondered what it was like to come into work and look at that all day. It must be enough to put you off sex: 'Oh God, not that again!'

Using the model, she demonstrated how the self-catheter was used. It looked pretty straight forward -especially on a plastic willy. 'I'm sure I can manage that.'

I figured I wasn't just going to get away with a theoretical demonstration, no matter how much optimism I displayed. And so it proved. Soon I was stripped from the waist down and pushing a plastic tube into myself. This was slightly smaller in diameter compared with what had gone before, and as a consequence it was a little easier. In it slowly went. Inch by inch. I half expected to feel it tickling the back of my throat. This task occupied both hands, and helpfully she was ready with a measuring jug. Then I paused:
'It won't go any further!'

I thought I'd been pretty calm, but sitting there with this long tube half-way into my body, my voice suddenly betrayed my anxiety. Bernie Bladder was starting to complain.

'It's ok Mr Meredith. You've reached the prostate. You need to push a little harder -push past the blockage. Give a little cough.'

I coughed it through. Then urine flowed. Elation was probably too strong a word, but I was quite proud of what I'd just achieved. A bit like those early prospectors when they struck oil. I was relieved. Firstly, because I'd been able to do something about the immediate pressure on my bladder. Secondly, I could see that with practice it was something I would be able to manage. It was never going to be easy, but wonder-weapon's encouragement would see me through. I was told to note down the volume each time. I'd regained some independence.

With catheters going in several times a day, the possibility of urinary tract infection was greater. I wasn't going to take any risks, so I popped into Lloyds Pharmacy to get some antiseptic wipes and lubricating gel. I waited around outside for some little time until the shop was reasonably empty -I didn't want the whole world knowing I needed lubrication. Then I buzzed up and down the aisles with my eyes flicking left and right. Then I zeroed in on my target. Made it look like I was picking up talcum powder and deftly changed direction at the last moment. The counter was clear. I homed in, furtively looking around:
'Umm. I'm buying this on behalf of someone else.'

There was a plain brown box by the front door. I wasn't expecting anything. Then I remembered my appointment with the nurse. These were probably my catheters.
Apart from its rather large size, the box was pretty discrete. An address panel. No labelling. Then I turned it over –'Medical Products' in large letters. It had probably been out here for hours. I hoped the neighbours might think it was a consignment of condoms. I wonder what the collective noun for condoms was? A stretch of condoms? Anyway, I digress. The delivery came with a glossy booklet. The photos showed young people with unblemished complexions leading impossibly fulfilling lives. Sharing a joke over a glass of champagne with some fabulous Caribbean beach as a backdrop; the sun just dropping out of view. They were just like me really. If I went to my local 'beach resort' at dusk and squinted a bit, I could pretend I was them. Especially if the oil storage tanks were burning off a bit of excess gas. I looked at them again. They must have had their hair dyed grey just for the photo-shoot. Then rushed off to rinse it out once the shoot was over. For these people, using a catheter was clearly a lifestyle choice.

'I can be aspirational too' I thought as I took a catheter out of its packaging.
First though, I thought I'd try something out. Only three months ago I could pass urine without any problem at all. Not large volumes, but enough not to arouse suspicion. I tried. Really tried. Nothing.
My reliance on the in-dwelling catheter meant that I was now unable to pass any urine at all. Without the support of the catheter, the urethra could no longer keep itself open against the pressure

of the enlarged prostate. I was now totally reliant on these disposable plastic tubes.

I sat on the toilet. I was about to have a deep and meaningful relationship with this plastic tube and all its other friends in the box. Well, maybe not meaningful but it would certainly be deep. According to my bladder, my catheter was my bestest friend. Better not tell wonder-weapon the news. It was ok though, I was used to managing complex relationships. I'd got four sisters. To each of them I'd send a birthday card and sign it with the words: 'You're my favourite sister. Don't tell any of the others'.

If I popped out to the shops, I'd pat my inside coat pocket to make sure I'd got a catheter with me. If I was an hour away from home and Bernie Bladder came calling, I could get into some difficulty without one within easy reach. I resisted the temptation to leave one discretely in my regular haunts. Didn't want the local tyre shop to go looking for my locking wheel nut tool, and discover something unusual in the glove compartment. They might start bleeding my brakes with it.

I left for work. Have I got everything? Coat. Security pass. Brain. Sandwiches. Oh, and my blue medical bag. I wasn't a functioning person without that.

Nobody gave me a second glance at work when I wandered off to the disabled toilet with my little blue bag containing my spare catheters, wipes and measuring jug. Surely someone must wonder what I had in there. Super soft toilet paper with my coat of arms printed on it? Maybe at my age they assumed it was a funnel. I suspected that they all knew the truth, but this kind of gossip was always spread with the prefix:

'Don't tell anyone else but....'

June would do something similar. If she was imparting a juicy bit of gossip her voice gradually reduced to a whisper. Then at the point that the meaty bit was about to be imparted, she would furtively look about, even though we were on our own and the person in question was a million miles away.

It wasn't my responsibility to pass on the good news at work. How could I? I could hardly drop the 'C' word into the conversation while making a cup of tea in the kitchen. Fit it in after discussing last night's football scores. I did have the odd moment when I wanted to unburden myself but it's not possible. It wouldn't be fair on people. Colleagues have a coffee in order to relax for a moment. Have a bit of banter. Let off steam. They don't want the worry of saying the wrong thing. I enjoyed a break as well, so I need to be prudent-otherwise I risked having the kitchen all to myself.

I'd read that some misguided people thought that cancer was contagious, so I didn't want my impending arrival in the kitchen to trigger my colleagues into scattering like a flock of sheep -throwing themselves head-first out of the windows.

I figured that people who stayed to talk to me:
- a) Didn't know I'd got cancer -and stayed to make ageist jokes.
- b) Knew I'd got cancer, realised it wasn't contagious, but still wanted to make ageist jokes.
- c) Knew I'd got cancer, thought it was contagious, but being adrenaline junkies, wanted to try it out for themselves.

I wasn't really bothered if the whole company knew. Cancer wasn't anything to be ashamed of. In fact, to use that cringingly fashionable phrase, it might 'raise awareness'. More importantly though, it might explain my occasionally vacant expression, although according to June I always looked like that.

In any company there was always a certain individual who made idle gossip a career option. Luckily, he was in my inner circle, and although I'd only hinted at my problems, I imagined he was taking care of business for me. I did wonder whether I should elaborate a little, I didn't want anything to get lost in translation. I remembered picking up my grandson from junior school:

'See those girls Grandad?

A couple of hand-holding girls had caught his attention. He looked up at me:

'They're Elizabethans.'

I'd never had cause to go into the disabled toilet before my illness, but I figured my current predicament improved my bargaining position. It was a palace amongst toilets. It was spacious and comfortable and I was eternally grateful for it. It was in a quiet location away from the facilities used by the peasantry. All joking apart, I needed some extra privacy, and the knowledge that my concentration would not be destroyed by an unexpected escape of gas in an adjacent cubicle. I was now becoming quite skilled with the self-catheter. It was a two-handed job, the measuring jug being held deftly between my legs, and I knew exactly when to cough. Most of the time it went according to plan. Sometimes, if my prostate was being particularly obstinate, no amount of coughing would persuade it to give way. On those difficult occasions, the only alternative to a trip to A&E was either to adjust your position or resort to the ultimate solution: push even harder.

Naturally, with my new-found freedom, I overdid it a little. I was up some obscure mountain in Snowdonia, freezing cold in a gale.

We're men - we can do these things. I'm at the top, about to punch the air in triumph, when Bernie Bladder comes calling. Because of the cold, love-pump is playing hide and seek. I lean back against the trig-point with my waterproof flapping against my face and get as comfortable as I can. I check I've got the place to myself. Once I've pushed the catheter in and it starts flowing, there's no way back. No way of turning off the tap. Not unless I pull the whole thing out fast - and I'm not doing that for anyone.

I check the wind direction for this sensitive task -I'm not a complete fool. Then, using my cold clumsy hands, I offer up the catheter-or would do if I could find the point of entry.

It was 14th March, and I was in hospital to sign the consent form for my prostatectomy. The nurse went through some basic questions regarding my health:

'Medication?'

I was pleased to be able to say 'No'.

'Dentures?'

Not so pleased to admit to partial one. My smile wasn't entirely my own.

'Eyesight? Do you need glasses?'

'No.'

Just at that point a heavy lorry passed by outside. It made quite a noise. I saw her lips move.

'Sorry I didn't catch that'

She smiled and repeated the question:

'Is your hearing ok?' No hearing aids?'

We both laughed. I guessed she must have heard that reply a million times, but she realised I genuinely didn't hear the question.

Then she went through all the risks. I was going to nod these through. Nothing was going to dissuade me from going ahead. It was a roll call of all that could go wrong:

Bloating, bleeding, bruising, hip and shoulder pain.
There was an interesting side effect. Because my urethra had to be stretched across the gap where my prostate used to be, there was a possibility that I could lose 'some length'.
I resisted a theatrical arm across the forehead and a cry of 'Oh thank God for that!'

On we went: Chest, wound and urine infection. Hernia, stricture, deep vein thrombosis, anastomotic leak and ileus. Injury to surrounding structures requiring a return to theatre.

This was becoming like the charge of the light brigade. On she went:
There was a possibility of conversion to open surgery if the robotic procedure didn't go according to plan.

The word 'incontinence' reverberated round the little room. Oh God – the 'dribbling' thing. I'd got used to being able to pee at my convenience, having some control. As for the 'pooping' thing -let's not even go there. It almost goes without saying that there was a risk of urinary incontinence. At the base of the prostate is a small sphincter muscle surrounding the urethra. This is what gives a man more bladder control than a woman, but with the removal of the prostate, this extra control follows it out of the door. A prostatectomy creates true equality between the sexes.

Still she charged on:

There was a possibility that if traces of cancer still remained, further treatment would be necessary and if that wasn't enough, stroke, heart attack and death.

My pen hovered over the form. She still hadn't finished. She saved the ultimate deterrent until last:
Impotence, loss of ejaculate and infertility. I'd pretty much anticipated these, but I would have appreciated it if she could have lowered her voice. If only out of respect. Wonder-weapon could hear everything.

So there it was -the full deck of cards, plus the joker.
I signed without a moment's hesitation.

It's beyond the scope of this book to explain these risks in detail but it gives you an idea of what you are willingly signing up to. A little while later I was back in hospital at the pre-admission clinic where various test were carried out. These included an electro-cardiogram and a blood test. They were checking that I didn't have any underlying problem that might prevent me from having the procedure. My bravery was not put to the test on this occasion.

Back home I looked down at wonder-weapon: Happy now? Unconstrained and free to roam he enjoyed a last hurrah. He deserved a nationwide tour, playing to sold-out venues every night, but I had never been able to get him the bookings, and that wasn't going to change now. My excuse was I had lawns to mow, the rubbish to put out. In any case I didn't have the necessary contacts. The reality was that he was a bit like one of those worn out pit-ponies that's allowed to spend his last few days on the surface, in the sunshine. Couldn't tell *him* that though could I? He thought he still had a star-studded future in front of him. I wasn't about to sit down with him, man to man, and have a discussion. What would I say? Where would I begin?

'Well Percy, we've had some good times together, but through no fault of your own you aren't going to be able to reach your full potential.'

'Sorry Love-Pump. I've never been able to give you the wide range of opportunities that your talent deserves.'

Maybe not. Anyway -we'd been a team. He'd never let me down, apart from showing too much initiative. But that was long ago. Now his career would be cut short by equipment failure. We had some good times and I knew life would never be the same again for either of us. I was running a closing down sale. As the day of the operation drew close, stock flew off the shelves. On the morning of the operation, I expected the bedroom door to burst open with a throng of fantasy acquaintances looking to grab never-to-be repeated bargains.

There was only one person more relieved than me on the eve of my operation. That was June.

If only. Like I say I had delusions of grandeur. I was hardly a rampant stallion. More like a nodding donkey. Especially if she wanted something doing. I couldn't get that carried away in the bedroom department anyway. As I got older, I realised that energy really is a finite resource.

It was the 28th March -the big day. Almost five months after my prostate biopsy it was pistols at dawn. My prostate or me. I was sat next to June in a waiting room trying to make light of things:

'I wonder if they could do a penis enlargement while I'm under?'

She had her sensible head on:

'Maybe they could get rid of that mole while at the same time -like two operations for the price of one!'
She put an arm round me:
'Don't worry B.D. -I love you just the way you are.'
There was a swish of curtains. My clothes were disappearing into a bag. On went my hospital gown and support stockings. I was told to wear the gown with the opening at the back. I did a quick twirl in front of June. If anything went wrong, I didn't want June's last view of me to be a toned and chiselled pair of buttocks. Or something like that. Probably more like one of those join-up-the-dot puzzles.

'Are you ok to walk Mr Meredith or do you need a wheelchair?'
I hated the wheelchair. You were literally being pushed around, trying to make conversation with your back to someone. There was always the risk of him tripping on a step, and tipping me into a rubbish chute. Anyway, I was happy to walk. I wasn't quite ready to surrender my independence. I didn't want a porter to get distracted, and deliver me to the wrong operating theatre. There were irreconcilable differences between me and my prostate. I didn't want to leave the building minus a perfectly healthy bladder only to find my prostate was still hitching a ride.
I walked down this corridor not knowing what to expect. A crowd of people in blue smocks forming a guard of honour? Bright lights? Fanfare of 'Ode to Joy?'

It was like a dream. I was trying to take in my surrounding but things were swimming about. I was invited to lie on a wheeled black-vinyl bed. The act of getting on to this was the point where I surrendered any ability to control events or effect what happened around me. It was warm – heated. Lying flat on your back puts the world in a new perspective. Everyone is higher up than you, and you can't meet the world eye to eye. I was in an ante-room being asked my name and date of birth. Boxes were being ticked. Then I was asked the most important and fundamental question of the whole exercise.

I understood about quality control. Fail-safe procedures:
'What operation are you about to have?'
It wasn't a trick question. I didn't need to phone a friend:
'Prostate.'

There was an injection in my wrist. Thirty-six years had elapsed since my one and only 'general'. Then I hadn't given it a moment's thought. I was young and fearless. Thirty-six years of being in complete control of events -well apart from the odd stag night and the thirty seconds of unconsciousness I suffered when I got knocked off my bike. I was willingly submitting to the ultimate state of helplessness. But I was ready. Here I go dear reader. Wish me luck.

The Operation

What are my test results?

You can use this section with your doctor or nurse to write down your test results and appointment dates.

PSA level at diagnosis: 30

Number of biopsy samples taken: 12

Number of biopsy samples affected: 4/6

Gleason score: G1 3+4 = 7

Grade group:

T stage at diagnosis (if known): T3a

N stage at diagnosis (if known): No

M stage at diagnosis (if known): Awaited

Date of MRI scan (if needed):

Results of MRI scan:

Date of CT scan (if needed):

My test results. Kindly filled in by my consultant.
Your life expectations distilled into seven lines of scribble

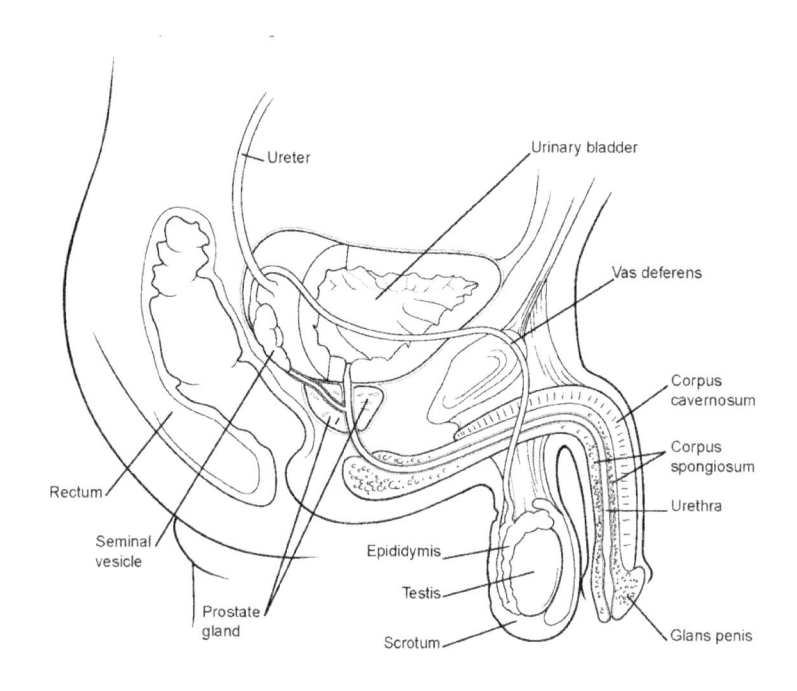

The Operation

Above:
The male reproductive system from the medical point of view.

Opposite:
The male reproductive system from the man's point of view

(*Compare this with the post operative view at the end of the next chapter. See if you can spot the differences!*)

The Operation

KEY:
1. Bladder
2. Seminal Vesicles
3. Urethra
4. Prostate
5. Penis
6. Testicles
7. Vas Deferens

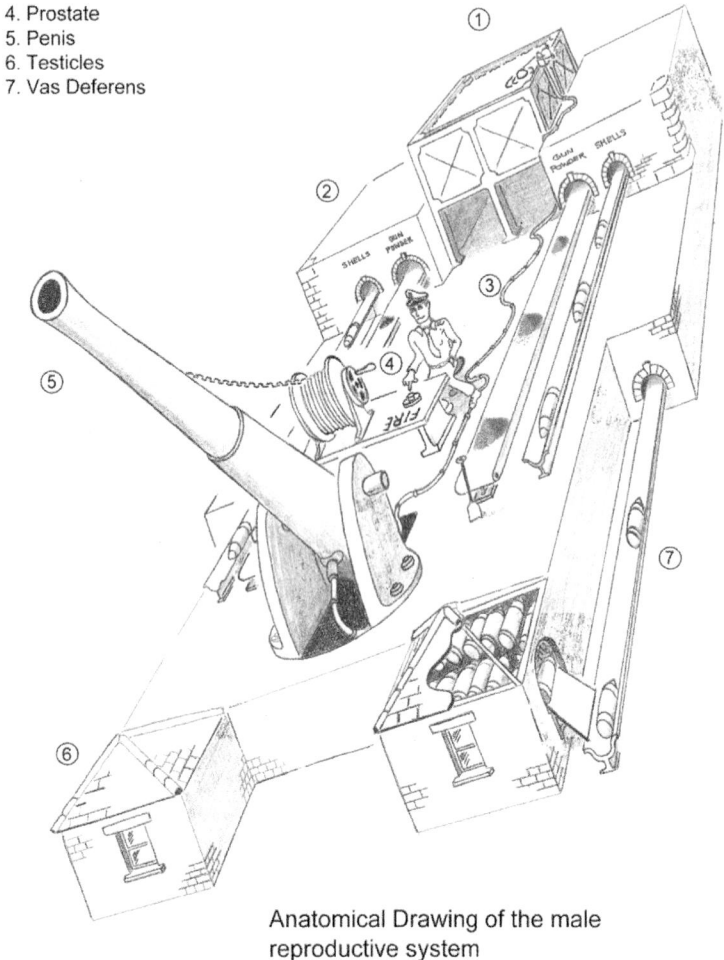

Anatomical Drawing of the male reproductive system
- from the man's point of view

8. The Operation

Of course. I have no recollection of this, so I will spend this chapter on the factors that influenced my decision making. I'm not offering advice here, and you should treat what follows with caution. It's just what I discovered **after** I made my decision. I guess I **could** have changed my mind based on what I discovered, but apart from a slight wobble or two, I stuck with my instinctive choice.

Let's get one thing straight here: it's very frightening to be diagnosed with prostate cancer, or any cancer for that matter. You're perfectly entitled to be fearful. Life isn't going to be quite the same afterwards.

Having said that, if you have prostate cancer then there are a whole range of treatment options. I remember the oncologist saying that if you were forced to have cancer then this would be the one to choose. If it was any relief to me, I'd chosen well. One disease - multiple cures. That was the good news.

However, the bad news (for some) is that the decision regarding which treatment option to go for is all yours. If, like me, you're used to passively accepting your fate when confronted by a medical professional, it can be a little disconcerting to have the ball thrown back at you. Welcome to the prostate cancer treatment buffet. A whole menu of options are available to you, and the urology team await your order. Of course the starter, a little appetiser known as a biopsy, is compulsory. Some might find all this choice empowering. Others will find the unexpected responsibility and range of options a little daunting.

If you're the kind of person who finds it a chore to shop around for the best energy deal, you may not enjoy this level of choice. Now wouldn't it be nice to be able to type your diagnosis into some kind of 'comparison website' and get survival rates for each of your options? Get it as an 'app' on your phone? Get busy Mr Zuckerberg.

There's a lot of information on the internet, but I'm not sure it helps. For every choice, there are heart-warming success stories and sad disappointments. If you are unsure (and who wouldn't be with this range of choice), then ask your urology team. They are dealing with this situation all the time, and their experience and advice is second to none. If you have a specialist urology or prostate cancer nurse at your hospital, they will be able to talk everything over with you, so do get in touch with them. Share with them any concerns you may have, and don't feel that you are being a nuisance. Of course, the time they can spend with you is limited, so try and be as well prepared as you can before you go in. This is an easy thing for me to say. Not so easy to carry out in practise.

The various booklets supplied by the NHS are regularly updated and should be the best advice you can get. I would urge you to read them from front to back.
If you can.
Whenever I tried to read the information given to me, I was confronted by an overwhelming feeling of dread. It was completely debilitating. I simply couldn't concentrate on the words written in front of me. Fortunately, I had one or two people I could talk to.

Don't expect your medical team to advise you which option to take. The ball is in your court. If you are offered a number of different options, it usually means that it isn't clear that one will be much better than another. Your urology team would be equally happy with whatever you decide. I think it's fair to say that all prostate cancer treatments have potential side effects, and these will be a major concern.

It might surprise you to know that the vast majority of men over eighty will have prostate cancer. For most of them it will be something they've had for many years. It will be slow moving and non-aggressive and the majority of them will die of other causes long before the prostate cancer becomes a problem.

If your cancer is not aggressive and is contained within the prostate, then you may not be offered any treatment at all. In this situation your doctor may recommend 'watchful waiting'. Also known as 'active surveillance'. This means that your cancer is actively monitored to ensure that it remains contained within the prostate. It will be a way of postponing treatment along with any potential side effects for the time being. It can seem counter-intuitive not to treat a cancer immediately, so it can take a while to get used to this idea.

With 'watchful waiting' you are choosing to leave the cancer in place when instinctively you want to be free of it. If you are given this option, it's clear you can take a little time in order to come to a decision.

'Watchful waiting' wasn't offered to me. Mine was T3a. It was breaking out. The stable door was already being pushed open.

Brachytherapy was not offered to me but is an interesting option. It's a treatment in which tiny radioactive 'seeds' are implanted in the prostate in an attempt to kill the cancerous cells inside.

The 'seeds' find their way into the prostate by…

No. I'm going to let you guess.

Do you really need me to tell you how they get there?

The Operation

Nice word 'implant'. Suitably vague. Like pushing seeds into potting compost. On the positive side it's an outpatient treatment, far less invasive than surgery, and statistics indicate that it is about as good at curing cancer as anything else. Wonder-weapon would have liked this one. No surgery, no catheter either. Still radiation though, so a reasonable amount of discomfort and side-effects. No cakewalk then, and you'd have to wait a couple of years while your PSA levels bounce around until they finally reach their 'nadir'. Only then could you be confident the treatment had been successful.

If the whole situation seems a little overwhelming that's because it is -at first, but will seem less so as you start to get to grips with the facts you are given.

Making the right choice when you have been given your options is quite a challenge. Don't expect any advice from me on this one. It's your body. You have to be comfortable with what you decide to do. The treatment options offered are determined by whether your cancer is localised, locally advanced or advanced. Depending on the stage of your cancer some items will be off the menu.

Mine was locally advanced. There were six possible treatment choices, luckily for me I was only offered two of these options. This was about as much 'choice' as I could cope with. I just wanted someone to put Humpty Dumpty back together again.

I remembered having breakfast in a downtown diner in Minneapolis when I was visiting my sister. I ordered breakfast. In particular, an American breakfast with coffee:

'Sure. How do you want your eggs? Over easy, sunny side up? Over hard? Medium? Basted? Coddled?
Coffee? Americano, Expresso, Latte, Cappuccino, Mocha......
How do you want your ham?'

By this stage choice had overwhelmed me. A queue was building behind me. I simply said yes to the last option in each case, because I couldn't remember what had been offered previously. Choice had bewildered and embarrassed me. Critically, choice put responsibility on *my* shoulders.

OK. Here we go. My choices were:

Surgery.
Or.
A combination of radiotherapy and hormone treatment. Because of my chronic retention, this option would also include a transurethral resection of the prostate. Commonly abbreviated to TURP. This was a procedure which involved opening up the part of the urethra which passes through the prostate.

I suppose I should have been grateful that a third option 'Kneel down and pray' hadn't been offered.

These treatments competed like rival car salesmen, trying to seduce me away from surgery with their optional extras.
Mr Radiotherapy could offer side effects like impaired sexual function, minor bowel problems and tiredness. Nothing new there. His colleague Mr Hormone-Therapy, was turning my head though. He could offer me exotic things I could only dream of like hot flushes and growth in breast tissue.
This got my attention, but although I'd always been quite self-reliant, having my own cleavage was probably a step too far. I really didn't want to bump into June on a clandestine visit to the lingerie counter at Marks and Spencer. I'd have to reveal who I was buying it for:

The Operation

I couldn't say 'you darling', my presence at the 38A end of the rack just wouldn't make sense.

I couldn't say 'me darling'. Secretly buying ladies underwear was a massive escalation in health risk. I could get hit by a frying pan.

If I panicked, and was stupid enough to blurt out 'somebody else', I would be considered a hopeless case and my medical team wouldn't want to waste any further time on me.

If that wasn't bad enough, muscle wastage was another one of his little treats. I really couldn't afford to lose any more. I'd just fitted some new brake pads on the car and had found it quite an effort to take the wheels off. I didn't want to face the truth, so I convinced myself that with each passing year, alloy wheels were getting heavier and heavier.

If things got any worse though, I wouldn't even be able to pick up the wrench. Hot flushes were another optional extra. June had these once. She was hot one minute and cold the next.

If you see a line of happy women with their backs to the wall, you can bet your house there's a radiator immediately behind them. I'd be joining them if I went for this one.

Then there was the TURP - This would also carry a risk of impaired sexual function, and would require a stay in hospital followed by several weeks of recovery just by itself. This was tipping the balance. Wonder-weapon preferred this but even he realised he might not be coming out to play so often. There were no easy answers here.

Surgery offered a better outcome in terms of survivability and how long you might expect to be cancer free. Even if your cancer was locally advanced, surgery wasn't always offered. Surgery promised a better outcome, and I was being offered the latest Robotic procedure as opposed to the more traditional 'open' surgery.

I was assured that with five small incisions rather than one fairly large one, I would benefit from a faster recovery. However, in the robotic procedure you are under anaesthetic for a considerably longer period of time. Typically for an open prostatectomy, you can expect to be under anaesthetic for 2 to 3 hours, compared with 4 to 7 hours for a robotic prostatectomy. I was 62 years of age and still running fifteen miles a week. I was advised that this wouldn't be a problem for me, but this may be a consideration for others.

After I informed the urology team of my choice, I had a brief period when I questioned whether I'd made the right decision. That's when all this information was gathered. Had I been hasty? I knew I hadn't fully explored the alternatives. I found all that difficult to cope with.

I knew which choice Love-Pump would have made. He would have liked the option that enabled him to come back out to play. But at what cost? Radiotherapy and hormone treatment could he hard on the body. I had a man-to-man talk with my bestest friend:

'This Radiotherapy, TURP and Hormones. Is it really worth it Wonder-Weapon?
Can I risk leaving the cancer in place?
Well?
Have you got anything to say on the subject?'

Not that I was going to pay any attention to his reply. Somebody had to be in charge, I couldn't let a 'minor appendage' dictate the destiny of the entire enterprise. I was calling the shots now.

The Operation

I'd like to say that I carefully considered both options, but with my family history my decision was driven largely by emotion. I chose surgery. A younger man might have different priorities, but it appeared to offer peace of mind. I would be free of the worry about what was actually going on down there. The alternatives were hardly a walk in the park, and I knew I would be continually worrying about whether anything had been missed. It put me a bit more in control.

I believed surgery to be the surest method of curing the cancer. It's a perfectly understandable motive to want to avoid the pain and inconvenience of surgery, and come away with the fewest side effects. The option of surgery appealed to my optimistic nature. After radiation treatment, few men report sudden erectile dysfunction. Over time, however, it becomes more common. However, after surgery, you will be left with an immediate erectile dysfunction problem that might well get better over time.

The hospital offered the Da Vinci Robotic System. Was this the best option for me?

Of course, by now I was googling frantically. I guess we all would in this situation, although I'm not sure how much help it is. Should I accept what I was being offered? An authoritative website offered the following help:

'..we encourage patients to choose an experienced surgeon they trust, and with whom they have rapport, rather than a specific surgical approach.'

Superficially this was quite useful advice but how was I supposed to act on information like this?

Were they on Facebook? Were there any performance tables? How was I supposed to make a judgement on rapport? Get them all in for an interview?

Was I in a position dictate terms? Choose which hospital? Which surgeon? Maybe I wasn't taking this seriously enough. Maybe I had to exercise my 'rights', whatever they might be.

Maybe I should put it out to tender -instigate a bidding war:

'Right, who wants my prostate?'

Sorry if I seem flippant. I fully understand that some people would want to explore their options, but for me there didn't seem to be any mechanism for me to exercise 'choice'.

I figured, maybe wrongly, that to properly explore the options, which surgeon, which hospital, which procedure, -would all take time, and so much had already drifted by. I didn't feel I had time to waste. I could be accused of acting emotionally I suppose, and if I am, then I'm guilty as charged. Me and my prostate had different priorities. It was personal. The time for mediation was past. It was me.

Or him.

When you're sat in front of a surgeon. The man who could save your life, it seems ungrateful, churlish, even slightly ridiculous, to start talking about 'choice'. Was I going to ask about his level of competency? His 'success rate'? My father and grandfather never had this opportunity. I was looking at the man who could save my life. He spoke quickly, almost hurriedly, but his confidence was infectious. I decided to place my trust in him.

So there you are. My advice is to try and stay calm. Consider your options carefully and come to a decision. Best not to follow my example and do it the other way around. Of course, sex is an important and enjoyable part of any relationship. You can be excused for giving too much consideration to the impact of the treatment on your sex life. It's not my intention to trivialise the sex thing. After all, when women start talking about sex, I've heard that while debate can get a bit heated over whether size matters, there's never any argument over firmness. No treatment gives absolute guarantees with regard to erectile dysfunction however, so focus on the treatment that offers the best cure for your cancer. Did you see what I did there? I jumped off the fence.

We must bring this chapter to a close. The Operation is over. The patient is being wheeled out of the recovery room.

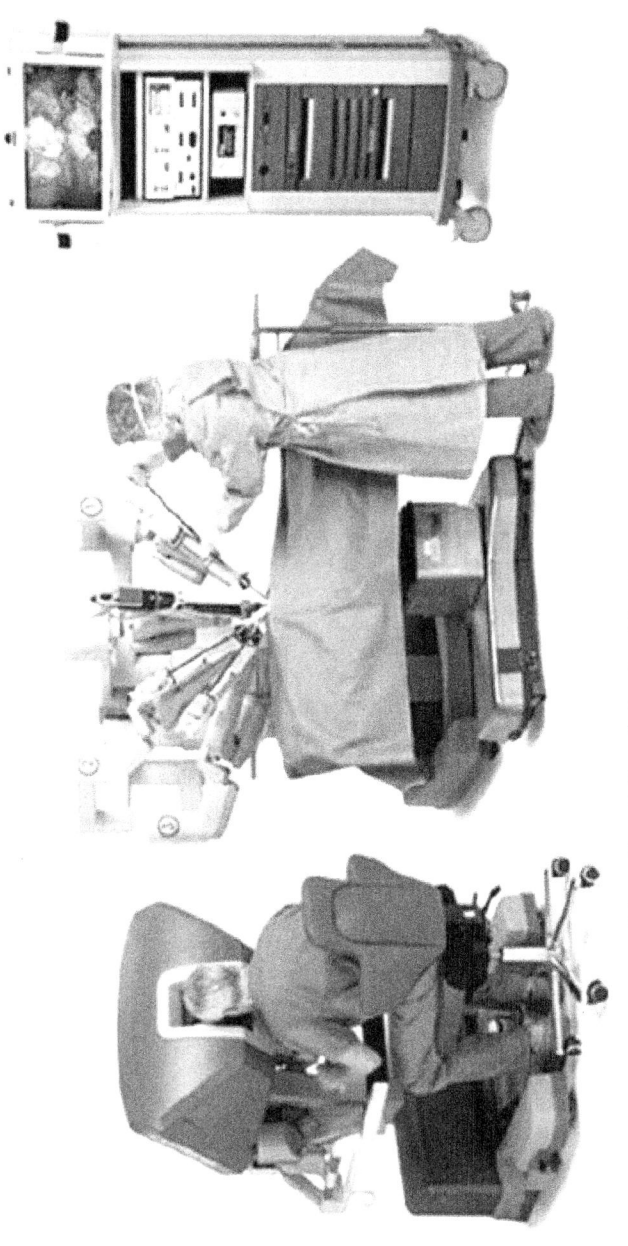

The Da-Vinci Robotic System

The Operation

Remnants of the male
reproductive system -post
operation
(compare with view at beginning of
chapter)

130

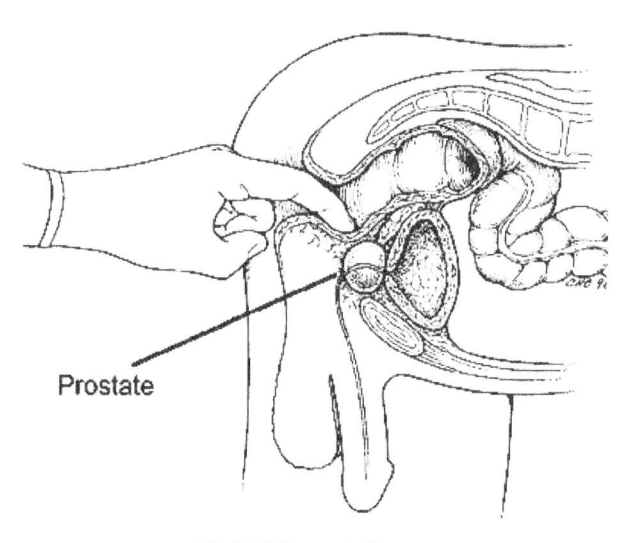

Digital Rectal Exam

9. Recovery

A light flashed. It swept across my field of view. Then there were more. Stripes of light rushed north to south. Noises. Then darkness and silence.

There was a bump. Then a strange noise. I'd never heard anything like it before, but then my brain went into retrieval mode and matched it with a squealing hinge. I wasn't just hearing and seeing now. I was making sense of my surroundings. A door-handle. Then darkness closed in again.

My eyelids were heavy, but up they came. I didn't realise it, but I was wriggling free of the anaesthetic. There was a gentle hiss in my ears. Things came into focus. People -other beds. I was seeing, but not really understanding my new surroundings. Then darkness again.

My body was coming back into action. Repair teams were busy. Upstairs I was getting green lights in the control room. A message flashed across the screen:
'Normal service will be resumed as soon as possible'.
Gradually I came back to life. I was relieved to discover that the hiss was caused by my oxygen tubes which had been routed over my ears. I drifted in and out of sleep.

I did a furtive kit inspection. My once finely tuned and taut abdomen looked like it had been machine-gunned by The Mob.
The catheter was back. A second tube came straight out of my stomach and headed away to a blood-tinged plastic bag. This would clearly have to come out at some point. That would be something to look forward to. A cannula on the back of my hand kept me

topped up with whatever I needed at that moment in time. Somebody had lifted me onto this bed, but at least I'd volunteered to do my own breathing. Apart from the drain tube, there were five other dressing across my stomach. My prostate had come out of one of these. I wondered whether it had put up much of a struggle. Five small incisions, a drain hole and a catheter suggested it did. Maybe it did an 'Alien' impression – erupting out of my stomach in five places before a panic-stricken medical team succeeded in skewering it with a surgical lance.

I expected some feedback on how the operation went. Maybe even a visit from the surgeon, but nothing was forthcoming. I wasn't expecting the nursing staff to stand at the bottom of the bed holding up scorecards, but some idea of what went on would be helpful. Maybe I could speak to someone who was there? Did the surgeon run around the operating theatre punching the air? Some spontaneous applause? A few tears maybe?
A nurse came to change the bottle on my cannula. The most that I could coax out of her was that the operation had gone according to plan. She did tell me that there would be an appointment with the surgeon at some point to discuss the results.

The ward was prepared for the night. A nurse swapped my leg bag for a night bag. I was aware of her by the side of the bed once or twice as the night wore on. Although the night was uneventful, I didn't sleep well. I had to stay alert. I imagined that someone could be along at any moment to prod something into me. I had to be ready to repel all boarders.

Light flooded into the ward. There was a shift changeover and then breakfast. I got talking to an elderly chap next me. He'd been in hospital for several weeks. There had been much scratching of chins at the bottom of his bed. The medical staff were trying to solve his problems. They were going to send him for a bone scan. Despite everything he was always cheerful.

'You can go to some dark places in here. Got to keep your chin up.'

The medical staff made their rounds. By early afternoon they were at the bottom of my bed.

'Have you slept well Mr Meredith?'

I lied.

'That's good. We'll take a few blood samples, and provided there's no problem you'll be going home today.'

After one night in hospital I was going home. Released again into an unsuspecting world. Over the next few hours, various bits of plumbing would be removed. June arrived in the afternoon.

'I can't believe they're letting you out after just one night.'

I wasn't unhappy about the prospect.

'It'll be fine.'

I was still drifting in and out of sleep. June had just been to her hairdresser and I was getting all the latest gossip.

'Don't worry if you feel like a sleep -I'll just keep talking.'

So I did. It was just like being at home.

I came to. A nurse appeared by my bed.

'I need to change your dressings Mr Meredith'

She moved towards my bed-sheet but I was already there -pulling it back. Then I was lifting my smock.

This was me; obstinately self-reliant. My default position if anything went wrong was to try and fix it myself. I'd spent my first week's wages as an apprentice toolmaker on a set of spanners, in order to fix a car I hadn't even bought yet. Fixing things myself was born out of necessity. My first daughter had arrived before I'd even

finished my training. Money had always been, as the songs says: 'too tight to mention'. I'd done every kind of car and home repair you could imagine. Things did get easier over the years, but self-reliance was a hard habit to break. It had been good to me domestically and had really paid off for me at work. Only quite recently, when I struggled with a wheel nut on a car, did I admit to myself that I really ought to offer this once-in-a-lifetime opportunity to someone else. June's idea of being pampered was a weekend in a health spa. Mine was a phone call from the garage saying:
'Mr Meredith -your car is ready for you to collect.' Bliss!

I was the kind of person who hated being fussed over. When I had my hair cut, I couldn't wait to escape the chair. I didn't like any restaurant which allowed the waiters to keep bothering you.
Right from quite a young age, I had been intent on taking care of myself. Being independent.
I first started earning pocket-money at nine years of age, when I started singing in a church choir. We'd get paid a little extra for singing at weddings, but Carol-singing at Christmas was a real money spinner. I was confident I could make more money operating freelance rather than in a group, and on more than one occasion I got invited into an old lady's house for a private recital. The best time to start was about ten days before Christmas. I'd discovered this the hard way the previous Christmas when, even before I'd even finished the first carol, a window opened high up in the darkness and I felt the impact of a penny coin. As I rubbed my sore head a voice rang out in the darkness: 'It's still bloody November for Christ's sake!'

As I watched the nurse change my dressings. I recognised that I could no longer do everything myself. At this moment I was utterly dependant on this woman's skill and care. I might be for some time. I now had to bow to the inevitable. It was hard for me to relinquish control and offer myself up into the care of somebody else. I was acutely aware of my limitations as I lay there on the bed. I was also humbled to be treated by someone who was clearly doing this out of a sense of vocation. She was a nurse with the NHS – it wasn't a get-rich quick scheme.
'That's looking good Mr Meredith!'
She looked at my drain bag.
'There's not much going on there now. I'll be back soon and we'll see if we can take that out.'
There was no mention of anaesthetic. I almost asked the chap next to me if he had heard the same thing as I did. This brave tube was going to have to come out all by itself. Without counselling.
Then she was back. I felt a cold antiseptic wipe on my stomach. She was calm. Professional. I trusted her.
'Breath in. Now breathe out slowly'.
As I did so I felt the strangest feeling. Not pain. More like discomfort. Like something was fluttering about inside my stomach:
'Oooh!'
'All done Mr Meredith. Just need to dress the wound.'
I watched her. She was busy with a scissors. Then a foil wrapper was opened. Something cold and damp on my stomach.
'Almost there.'
I caught sight of her identity badge. She was about to go.
'Emma?'
She looked up. I caught her eye:
'Thanks.'
She paused for a second and smiled. Then she was gone.

Later a plaster appeared where my cannula used to be. I was being readied for lift off.

'We just need to do your Fragmin injections then you're ready to go.'

I was now battle-hardened. An injection? Bring it on.

Two fully-qualified nurses appeared at my bed. I had now got over my 'white coat syndrome' and could identify the various ranks within the nursing profession. In particular, the distinction between those who could 'insert' and those who were restricted to 'measuring'. In a hospital where qualified staff were at a premium, this was unusual and should, by itself, have raised the alarm. One 'measurer' was fine, but two 'inserters' hinted at back-up, restraint and morale support. I should have suspected something when they drew the curtains. It all started to go wrong when the nurse handed the actual injection to me. Were we playing doctors and nurses? I handed it back:

'Yeah nice.'

Then it was back in my hand again. She held another in her own hand. The safety cap came off with a 'pop'.

I was clearly expected to copy what she was doing. I pulled the cap off. The needle wasn't too long, but it was very small in diameter. I could hardly bear to look at it. I wondered where it was going next. I resisted the foetal position.

'Now pinch the skin at the top of your thigh. Make a fold in the skin.'

I still hoped that she just wanted some co-operation with this injection. Of course! That was it! I was just helping out.

I pinched some skin.

'You need to relax your leg Mr Meredith. Straighten it out.'

I was now able to pinch a big fold of skin. I pulled it away from the muscle beneath.

'Now inject into the fold'.

OH MY GOD.

There could be no doubt now. I was going to have to push this thing into me. Half of me wanted to be brave in front of all these women. The other half resisted this needle with every fibre of its being.
I placed the needle against my leg and pushed. There was a depression in the skin. I pushed harder. Shaking now, the needle looked like a pole in a tent.
'I can't do it!!'
'You're doing fine Mr Meredith.'
I really wasn't. If I was doing 'fine' how on earth would they define 'not fine'? I was sweating. Holding my breath. Maybe they would give up soon and do it themselves.
I pushed a bit more. My breath came to me in gulps. Oh God, I was getting emotional. Everyone outside the curtain can hear me and I'm losing it. My forearm can feel the resistance. Then suddenly it's going in.
'All the way in Mr Meredith.'
Then the resistance dropped. My stomach turned over: I was obviously through the skin and into the void behind.
'Now push steadily on the plunger.'
I battled to hold everything steady. The plunger moved down the tube.
'Now take it out straight.'
Keep calm. Home straight. Don't break the needle.
'Thank God that's over.'
I was relieved. My thigh had put up quite a fight. The nurse handed something to me.
'There you are Mr Meredith...'
I was holding a box.
'...a month's supply.'
You can't be serious!

Recovery

A box full of injections. The implications were immediate and obvious. I was going to be sticking these things into myself for quite a while. By the time I looked up they were gone.
A month's supply!
I wish it had been February. They returned shortly with some paperwork.
'After a few weeks you'll get an appointment for the removal of the catheter and stitches. Here's a leaflet about the pelvic floor exercises. It's important to do these. They will help you get control of your bladder once the catheter is removed.'
'Sorry about.. well..just now. I'm not very good with injections.'
She smiled.
'The first is always the worst. You'll be ok. You might find it easier to inject into the stomach. It's important to take the whole course. They protect you against blood clots.'

I was fine with injections as long as I didn't have to see the needle going in. Now, not only would I now have to see, I would have to *feel* as well.
Did I know anyone in the nursing profession who fancied a little freelance work? Anyway, what would be the going rate? I'd quite happily pay someone fifty quid to do it, but there were nearly thirty of these things. There was really no choice. I was somehow going to have to get past this problem.
I was glad that I had succeeded as an engineer. After my experience with the Fragmin, I knew I would never have made it as a drug addict.

Back at home, I focussed on the leaflet and did my pelvic floor exercises. When you're young you hardly know where this muscle group is -you're too busy concentrating on your abdominals and biceps. It's understandable. You get the girl by standing squarely in front of her, popping on your shades, flashing a whitened smile and displaying a rippling six-pack. I'm not speaking from personal experience of course. I got the girl by looking like I needed help. My appeal was to her caring side. I've never had a second glance. The only way I'll get one now is by walking into an operating theatre 'open at the back'.

The leaflet explained exactly which muscle I needed to exercise and how to do it. If I exercised the wrong muscle, I risked having a wonderfully toned abdomen, only to ruin it with a rapidly increasing damp patch further down. No. I made sure I exercised the **right** muscle. Anyway -this might have long term benefits. I figured a lady of a certain, let's say **distinguished** age, is going to be pretty impressed by me popping on my varifocals, flashing my dentures and showing off a perfectly toned and chiselled pelvic floor muscle. You might need to adopt a pretty odd position to display this effectively, and you might risk being stuck in this position for some time. But no. I think it's worth it. A discerning woman will see the benefit straight away: no mattress protector.
I now set out to break the world record water-tightness time post-operation. I was on a mission.

Morning again. Our familiar bedroom. Clouds scudded across the sky. I looked over the side of the bed. The return of the bed bag, only now the straw colour had changed to reddy/brown. This was to be expected for a while apparently. My first thought was the injection. It was my second thought as well. In fact, I could think of nothing else. I had to face it. Come up with a plan. I drew a calendar. Thirty boxes representing my daily Fragmin injections. I coloured in yesterday's jab. Immediate progress. I would do today's straight after breakfast. Well maybe just before lunch. This became tea time. It was my only task of the day and it was going to occupy my thoughts **all** day.

'Have you done your jab yet?' asked June as she got ready for bed.
'Oh no. I've completely forgotten. Thanks for reminding me.'
It was now or never. I went off to the spare room.
'If I'm not back by tomorrow morning, send out a search party.'
'Good luck.'
'Thanks. Don't disturb me.'

I needed to fully concentrate on this. An unexpected noise could be disastrous. If only I could have a local anaesthetic -but who else was around to administer it? Maybe twenty consecutive episodes of 'Teletubbies' could be relied on to achieve a suitably soporific state. 'Emmerdale' would be quicker though.
I got busy with the antiseptic wipe. Then out came the injection. As soon as I heard the 'pop' of the safety cap I was back in the hospital, shaking again. A battle of wills ensued. I pinched some skin. Pushed. Pushed some more. Gave up. Tried again. This pushing and shoving took a little time. The Devil was in my ear:
'Just put the needle in the bin. No-one will ever know.'
If that wasn't enough, there was a civil war going on in my forearm. Muscles loyal to me were pushing this needle in as best they could. Other muscles loyal to me, were putting up fierce resistance. Ten minutes later I'm still trying. I Push. Push a little harder. The point of the needle is lost in a pit of skin. I grit my teeth. Hold my breath. Slowly increasing the pressure.
I'm in!
The view makes me slightly faint.

Breathe out. I keep pushing the needle in. Then a sudden drop in resistance.

'Uuuh!'

I was through, into the void between the skin and the muscle.

Hold it steady.

Push the plunger nice and slow.

Withdraw nice and straight.

Then I safely disposed of the needle in a yellow plastic box. Or 'sharps' box as they say in the business.

My squares gradually filled up with colour. Eventually the coloured squares outnumbered the blank ones. Each square was an achievement. I have a folder with all my appointments. It's like a diary of my illness. At the back is a piece of lined paper with coloured squares.

I'm on three coloured squares. I've had cancer, and the bedroom remote is all mine. This won't last of course, but I'm in dependency mode and I let the TV wash over me. After a couple of days though, the attraction begins to pall. Another Emmerdale catch up.

Another opportunity for those who didn't understand the plot the first time around.

Ah! 'Emmerdale'. I'm convinced that every script is just a cut and paste re-arrangement of the previous episode. The latest opus finished with the words:

'If you have been affected by Chas and Paddy's story you can visit http://www.itv.com/advice for support information'

My curiosity is aroused, so I'm there in a flash, but all it consists of is a list of various help groups dealing with everything from breast cancer to managing transgender children. Although prostate cancer is the third biggest cancer killer in the UK, there's no mention of it. It doesn't exist in 'Emmerdale'. The biggest threat to a man in 'Emmerdale' is to run out of plot lines, after which he is unceremoniously despatched in the woods behind Home Farm.

I guess the Emmerdale production team know their audience. Unfortunately, there's no help group for those who are 'affected' by its sheer awfulness.

Not that I watch it of course -it just happens to be on. It's making me a grumpy old man. I need to break the cycle, and I will -once I've watched 'Cash in the Attic'.

Ah! 'Cash in the Attic'. I tried to avoid programmes like 'Jeremy Kyle'. I suspected these programmes were intentional poor -their aim being to force the unemployed and sick back to work.

June was doing the supermarket shop. I had assured her I would be alright in her absence.

'Do you want anything?'

'Only your safe return' I grovelled.

Half an hour later I'm experiencing a pain in my lower stomach. I think about a pain killer. It fades away. Some Ming Dynasty vase, bought by one of the contestants for £3, is about to be auctioned. The pain comes back. It folds me up. I toss and turn trying to find a bearable position. The auctioneer's gavel comes crashing down but I can't see it. I'm on the floor, my eyes are screwed shut and I'm smelling the carpet.

The pain goes away. I get back into bed, a bit shaken by the whole experience. Of course, now the pain has gone I assume I can ignore it. I'm a man. I'll just take a few painkillers -at some point. Once I find out what that vase went for.

The pain's back. Increasing. I'm on the floor again. It's so bad now I can't localise it. I can hardly think. I hear the front door. A voice. My name. I can only pant. Someone climbing the stairs. They're at the door looking at an empty bed. I'm out of sight on the floor at the far side. She's off across the landing calling my name. I inch across the floor. My every exhalation is accompanied by a moan. She hears me and comes back.

'Oh my God -what's the matter?'
I'm panting words: 'pain -down -here'.
I knew I was well beyond an aspirin now.
'Right, I'm taking you to A&E'
I've got myself to the car. I'm in full man-pain mode. We're stuck at traffic lights. I'm wondering if I'm going to get to hospital in time.
'Oh God -h-hurry up!'
Then we're off again.
More lights. We're at the back of a queue. There's a left turn filter-lane. Empty.
'Go up the inside and jump the lights.'
'I can't do that!'
I'm panicking now.
'Just f*cking do it!'
Thankfully she ignores me.
We're moving again, along familiar roads. But they look somehow different -as if everything is receding away from me. I'm reaching out as if I'm trying to hang on to it all.
'If....If I black-out..'
I was panting loudly. Despite everything I knew if I lost consciousness, I would lose control of events.
'..don't let them take...my catheter out.'
It was allowing my urethra to heal onto my bladder without the agitation of urine. I'd gone through too much for that to be disturbed now -even by accident.
We dispensed with roadside parking and pulled up alongside ambulances coming and going outside the entrance to A&E.
Just a few steps to go. I thought I would pass out at any moment. Then I'm slumped at the counter relying on June to do the communication. Another Oscar-winning performance. Well, I've broken the cycle -my brief addiction to daytime TV. But not in the

way I'd planned. June later told me A&E hadn't been too busy, and I'd been able to go straight in. I have no recollection.

Patients are quietly going about their normal lives -being ill and getting treated. Suddenly this noisy exhibitionist comes in demanding attention. Except I wasn't demanding verbally – I could no longer speak.
Curtains swish. An injection goes in. The pain subsides. Tears well in my eyes. A beautiful, calming and peaceful injection -morphine. Within minutes, I'm sitting in a chair next to the bed. June recognises a former work colleague nearby. She's brought her elderly father in with a problem. She did tell me what it was, but I was too busy apologising for the racket I must have made. Anyway- I'm in a little bubble of euphoria, and despite appearances to the contrary, I'm not really there. Then June leaves to park the car in a sensible place and I'm moved into a ward. I drop off to sleep. Of course, I'm in a fool's paradise. The pain has been relieved temporarily, but the underlying problem is still there.

June arrived later with some home comforts. I apologised for my outburst in the car.
'Well you were in a lot of pain.'
That was indeed true. I hadn't suffered like that since Cheltenham got relegated two years ago.
I pointed to my leg-bag:
'I'll be back in a minute.'
I found the toilet just off the ward. The light was flickering so badly in the toilet, that it effectively put it out of use. A nurse directed me to another further down the corridor:
'We're waiting for someone to come out and fix it.'
I returned to the ward.

'You were a long time.'
'The toilet is out of order for the want of a light bulb.'

Later, after June had left for home, a nurse arrived to check my catheter.
'Somebody said that the catheter could be irritating the neck of the bladder' I ventured.
'It's possible' she replied, 'but for now let's just get some rest.'
Nobody was going to tell me what had been the cause of my pain. They operated on a 'need to know' basis, and I didn't need to know. Ignorance is bliss, and I'm happy to co-operate on that basis. Of course, the problem is still there, masked by morphine, but I didn't waste much time thinking about it.
Another nurse arrived at my bedside to give me my medication and take blood samples. I was finding the Fragmin injections difficult, and I thought I'd ask an expert:
'Is there a technique to doing these Fragmin injections?'
'Are you having problems?'
'Well. It just takes me ages to..you know..get the needle in.'
She looked across at the next bed.
'I'll be giving Mr Taylor a Fragmin later. I'm sure he won't mind if you want to watch.'

Mr Taylor. So that was his name. Even in the short period of time that I'd been in the hospital, he had established himself as a bit of a character. The chap in the bed opposite, said that he had American Red-Indian ancestry, and his Indian name was 'Walking Wind'. He was certainly living up to that. He was about my age, and had established quite a rapport with the nurses, to the extent that there was some friendly competition for the right to do his injections. He had been in hospital for several weeks, but was going home later. I was slightly in awe of him. He had obviously succeeded in obtaining something I didn't even have the nerve to ask for: He had charmed the nurses into administering his Fragmin injections. I was looking forward to learning something.

Well the hours ticked by. Monotonous hours of inactivity interspersed with occasional moments of (usually unpleasant) high drama. Mr Taylor was dressed and ready to leave, and sure enough the nurse arrived with her yellow 'sharps' box and injections. The nurse threw me a glance, while I made myself comfortable on the edge of the bed. Had popcorn been available I would probably have bought some. 'Walking Wind' was beaming from ear to ear as he lifted up his t-shirt to expose his stomach. There was the familiar 'pop' of the safety cap and in one movement the nurse appeared to just pat him on the stomach. Then I heard a clatter in the bottom of the 'sharps' box.

I sat there waiting for something to happen:
'All done Mr Taylor!'
I was incredulous: 'You're kidding me! Is that it?'
I leant forward.
'Can you do that again? I missed it!'
He laughed.
I wouldn't have believed it if I hadn't seen it with my own eyes.
'Do you want me to do yours now Mr Meredith?'
'Er no. If that's alright. You don't play darts by any chance, do you?'
She smiled and was gone. I heard Mr Taylor's laugh echo down the corridor. I looked at the chap opposite:
'He seemed to be happy to be going home.'
'Things aren't always as they seem. I was chatting to him yesterday, after they told him he could go. He's dreading it. He's going home to an empty flat. In here he's got people to talk to, he's well looked after.'

Another night. Another day. It became apparent that I was running a temperature and wouldn't be allowed to return home until it had stabilised. Actually, staying in hospital was bearable, almost enjoyable, for someone like me who didn't actually *feel* ill. People attended to my every whim and desire. My niece called by at the end of her twelve-hour shift to wish me well. She looked exhausted. I almost offered her my bed.

My elevated temperature meant there was clearly a battle going on somewhere, but as long as they didn't poke me with anything, then ignorance was bliss. Uniforms gathered at the foot of my bed every morning to exchange frowns, while I occupied myself with the lunch menu.

After three days my temperature had stabilised. My kidney function was ok. There was another complication that I tried my best not to think about, but despite this I'd been told I could go. I'd been given the nod of approval. I used to gaze out of the ward window watching people go about their everyday lives. I was about to re-join them. My catheter was working normally, but for three days there had been a noticeable lack of activity at my waste disposal chute. This was a common side effect of morphine -your bowel goes to sleep. Mine was becalmed – there wasn't a breath of wind. I'd got friendly with the chap opposite. He advised me to speak to the nurse:

'We'll give it a few more hours and if nothing has happened, then speak to me again.'

I wanted to be sure everything was good in the number two exit corridor before departing for home. I was thinking about my bucket list, and I was in the mood to cope with anything she might throw at me. Time ticked by without activity. I might be going home in an hour. The nurse returned to the ward. I caught her eye. There was a swish of curtains.

'Lie on your side Mr Meredith –try and relax…'

About half an hour later I was heading to the loo. A few months ago, the bottom had fallen out of my world. Now the world was falling out of my bottom: My first enema.

June arrived. I was on my way. We were packing away my bits and pieces.

'Where's your sick note?'

I hadn't got one. I'd been able to self-certify for the first five days, but now I would need some kind of proof, if I was to continue to get paid. Questions were asked. Soon afterwards a doctor appeared by my bedside.

'How long will you be off for' she asked, holding a form in her hand. This was like being presented with a blank cheque, but I resisted the temptation.

'My employer isn't expecting to see me for four weeks.'

Her pen flashed across the form and she was gone.

I read it carefully. I would be handing it in to our HR department and I wanted it to be correct.

'Well well well!'

'What's up' asked June, looking at the form.

Under 'cause' I was expecting to see 'Prostatectomy' but instead I saw the word: 'Sepsis'.

'So *that* was the cause of the pain.'

'I don't care now' I said, waving my sick note around like Chamberlain at Munich,

'I've got four weeks off work to recover.'

'What's this?' June asked, picking up a blood test form.

'My liver function isn't right.'

She frowned.
'I know. I'm trying not to worry about it.'
We gathered up my things. After three days I was on my way home. I was all smiles. We walked past the toilet door. The light was still flickering.

We were getting ready for bed. My finely tuned and muscle-hardened body came into view. I could boast that I still wore thirty-two waist trousers – I just wasn't pulling them up so far. I got my bed-bag sorted out. I stood there in my support stockings, my catheter snaking seductively down my leg. My wound plasters shimmered bewitchingly in the moonlight. June looked up:
I peeled back a bit of support stocking. Exposed some naked flesh.
'Phwoar! What a body!'
'Yeah – be great when it's finished!'
I got into bed. She drew close to me:
'Let's do something reckless.'
I smiled. One day the train might enter the tunnel again. But not under its own steam, and not just at the moment.
'Come on -whip me into a frenzy!'
I looked at her:
'You might need to join a self-help group.'
She tried to be supportive:
'They say it might take up to twelve months to fully recover -you never know. It might come back one day.'
We both lifted the duvet, and looked down at what was left of one of the greatest woman-pleasing features known to mankind -after the credit card and the oven-cleaner of course. Superficially, my wonder-weapon still seemed to carry latent threat. The munitions factory was still there, but the hoist taking the shells to the magazine had been cut years ago. Now I've had the op, not only are

there no shells, but there's no magazine and no propellant. It wasn't a question of there being no one in the control room to operate the pulley to get wonder-weapon into firing position - there wasn't even a control room any more.

No one was running things on my behalf down there. I was now in full control of the entire operation. Previously, there had been a battle for power. Sometimes wonder-weapon had usurped my authority with disastrous results. In fact, women were convinced there was no executive control at all, and that wonder weapon was running the entire enterprise.

June lowered the duvet, solemnly:

'Shall I go and get some TCP?'

My coloured squares were getting more numerous. The injections left tell-tale bruises on my leg. After a few of these I switched to my stomach. I found it slightly easier. There was no reduction in resistance as you got through the skin. No bruising either. I marked each site with an indelible pen so I wouldn't return to the same place. My stomach was a patchwork of circles and dressings.

Tempting thoughts entered my head. Maybe I could just do twenty. Surely that would be enough. No one would know. I was answerable only to me. Not a good place to be when resilience and determination was required. I remembered a work colleague had been in hospital for an operation recently and I wondered how he had coped with the injections.

'I wasn't finding it easy either Dave so I spoke to my Doctor.'

'What did he say?'

'He said 'Well it's your body. Your life"

I had my answer. That was quite unequivocal. 'Keep going then' I thought to myself.

'So what did you do then?' I asked.

'I just stopped after a week.'

This just made more determined to get through to the end. I'd got this far. I wasn't going to stop now.

No matter how much I rested, blood in the urine persisted. I was due to have the catheter removed two weeks after the operation, and I was sure they wouldn't take it out unless the urine was clear. Just over a week after the operation, I woke to discover my leg bag was a golden straw colour. I continued to rest, but buoyed by my clear urine, I was feeling pretty good. The following day my support stockings hit the bin. I wanted a bit of normality. Wanted to prove to myself I could recover quicker than anyone else. Normal recovery times didn't apply to me. I didn't want to overdo it though. I wasn't going to do something reckless, like picking up June's handbag.
'I'll give the inside of your car a sweep out' I said to June.
'Are you sure that's a good idea?'
'Yeah. It'll be fine. Got to start doing **something**.'
I was quite pleased with myself. I'd managed the bending and stretching without any discomfort.
The car was spotless.
Later I looked at my leg bag. My urine was back to reddy/brown.
'Oh!'
'Trust you to overdo it' June told me when I confessed later.
I felt such a fool. It was going to be rest, rest, rest from now on. Hopefully things would return to normal.
I sat down looking at some old photos. I found my black and white christening photograph again. Like me it was a bit tired round the edges. There I was, bringing happiness and joy to so many people - without even trying. Where did it all go wrong?
Then June was making a phone call. She was talking to her brother Brian. He'd also undergone a prostatectomy in the recent past, but

was about a year in front of me in terms of recovery. He was already experimenting with vacuum-pumps, injections and little blue tablets.

'Yes Brian. I told him not to do it.'
A telling-off was on its way. My body was already folding up into the foetal position.
'Don't worry, I'll pass your message on' she continued:
'I'll tell him not to be such a pillock.'
Then there were the words I had been dreading:
'Ok Brian. Thanks very much.'

These words signalled the end of the phone call, and the moment my admonishment would begin. I needed to look busy. I rushed into some pelvic floor exercises.
'I take it you heard that.'
I nodded:
'Can't talk.' I said between gritted teeth: 'Pelvics.'
'He says you've just had a major operation, and you have got to rest every hour of the day. You'll be back in hospital if you're not careful!'
I was glancing at my watch and holding my pelvic floor muscle in tension. I gave June a tight smile and a thumbs up.
'Oh have it your way -you'll learn.'
They didn't need to say any more. I had learnt my lesson.
In just a few days I was due to have the catheter removed as part of a 'trial without catheter' procedure. It was essential that my urine was clear. I went straight to bed. Another morning and I was relieved to see it return to normal. I was a good boy in other ways: I was doing my pelvic floor exercises like my life depended on them. June knew when not to bother me. I had my 'constipation' face on.

Nobody had said much up until now but suddenly cards arrived every day. June had unwittingly taken on the role of press officer, dealing with the delicate issue of regular news bulletins and managing reactions. Only with the arrival of all these cards did I realise what a benefit this had been to me. Spared from the communication task, I was able to focus all my energy on staying positive. Of course, had I been facing the 'managed exit', this role would have been critical, well-meaning enquiries into my bone-scan result being something of a conversation stopper.

There were cards from family, close friends and even people I hadn't spoken to for years.
I even had a card signed by all the players in my skittles team.
There was a knock at the door.
Some words were exchanged and June returned with a bouquet of flowers. She had a smile from ear to ear.
She pecked me on the cheek:
'Thank you darling!'
I admit I was a bit puzzled.
She walked away from me, smelling the flowers while opening up the accompanying card.
'Oh!'
Her face dropped:
'They're for you!'
Blimey, who was giving me flowers? I looked at the card:
'From all your colleagues at Sandy Coloured Boxes.'
I knew it was just someone in HR doing their job, but it was still really touching.

Recovery

It was the 10th April, I was in hospital for my 'Trial without catheter'. I lay on the couch while nearly thirty stitches were removed. Another entry on my bucket list. They looked like the kind of large staples you'd find on an IKEA package. Despite this I was pretty relaxed. A year ago I would have lost sleep over this, but after all I'd been through I was confident I could manage the situation. And so it proved. In ten minutes, most of them came out without any complaint at all. Then the nurse removed my fifth and final catheter. This came out relatively easily. Not as easy as accidentally signing up for Amazon Prime, but certainly more comfortable than in the past.

With my stitches gone, my catheter gone and free of my support stockings, I felt like a butterfly emerging from its chrysalis. I wanted to discover what my new body could do. Test my wings -or at least test my new plumbing arrangements. I sat there in close contact with my new friend, the incontinence pad. There were a number of us sitting around drinking water at regular intervals. When we felt the urge, we'd wander into an adjacent room, where a piece of equipment suspended in a toilet measured the amount of urine being passed. In that room we'd remove the pad and try and urinate normally. A nearby printer would come to life and record the volume and pressure on a piece of graph paper. We sat around making supportive noises – waiting to see which candidate would be first to wake the printer up.
I sat there quietly drinking. Then I felt a familiar feeling. I stood up, and as I did so I felt myself leak uncontrollably. I couldn't stop myself. I had nothing to stop myself with. Too late, I remembered my pelvic floor exercises.

By the time I got to the measuring device I didn't need to go anymore. The printer was silent. I shrugged my shoulders in front of all the other contestants and returned to my seat. An hour later I tried again. Attempt two was a little better – a bit of a trickle. Some of the men had already rushed into the nurse waving their print-outs like schoolchildren handing in their homework. They had been sent home like boys who had finished their detention.

Then I was in an adjacent room where a nurse performed an ultrasound scan of my bladder. She sensed I needed some reassurance:
'Empty!'
My bladder was completely empty for the first time in years. This meant my kidneys were performing more effectively and safely. Then I returned to drinking and measuring. Two of us left.

Of course, having both been through the same experience, we exchanged Gleason scores. Started discussing illness and dryness. Not firmness, we didn't know each other well enough for that. It transpired that he had entered the operating theatre just a few hours after me.
He had been diagnosed more recently than I had, but had shortened the timescales by going private on his biopsy. I was curious:
'I suppose it's less worry, less risk of it spreading if you can speed things up?'
'Not so much that - I'm taking my yacht round the Baltic. This holiday has been a year in the planning. I didn't want to miss out on it.'
I liked his style. He saw prostate cancer as a minor inconvenience that had to be batted out of the way so he could go on a pre-

arranged holiday. I would have considered this course of action if I had been aware of the possibility. I drew some comfort from the fact that despite the expense, I'd beaten him to the operating table by a few hours.

It was just starting to get interesting when Bernie Bladder butted into the conversation. Then I was in front of the measuring device again. For the first time in five months I was passing water naturally and hitting the mechanism with a little pressure. I was so relieved to see this happening again. If I had been on my own I might have run around the room punching the air, my incontinence pad flapping around my ankles. Like flushing a loo, or releasing a plug in a bath, they are things you don't give much thought to, until for some reason they stop working. The printer burst into life and shortly afterwards I was whistling down the corridor with a packet of incontinence pads under my arm.

I went to bed with my new sleeping partner, the incontinence pad. I was woken several times with the urge to take a leak but on each occasion, very little came out.
The following morning, I woke up and immediately checked the incontinence pad -dry. This was too easy surely? I was hoping for a fast resolution to the dryness issue but even in my wildest dreams I didn't expect to be continent so quickly. Smugly, I decided to go for a walk -without my pad. I bent over to tie my laces. I felt a slight dribble.
I wasn't discouraged. I set off across the fields. Enthused, I sprang over a stile like a gazelle. Landing on the other side I felt a dribble. A few metres further on, another drip. The situation was bewildering because there were no signals from Bernie Bladder. No

pattern to the drips. There would be a few steps and a drip. Then nothing for a few hundred metres. Then a big dribble.

Half a mile further on I felt damp and miserable. I decided to return home. Suddenly, I had a lump in my throat and I was fighting back tears. I wanted to disown my failing body, take it back for a refund. Revoke my decision to have surgery.

As I despondently trudged across the field with my spreading damp patch, I realised what an impact incontinence would have on my life. I'd have to carry a 'man bag' full of new and used incontinence pads about with me. I'd have to change my drinking habits, take clean clothes everywhere. In public places I'd have that constant worry about the smell of urine. Then I thought of all the things I would no longer be able to do. Before my operation I used to cast envious looks at joggers as I passed them in the car, hoping that one day I'd be able to re-join them. This would be difficult if I had to carry a bag of pads and underwear.

I could see myself retracing my route in the car after a run -picking up pads that I had tearfully discarded along the way.

I had been fooled by the incontinence pad's wonderful ability to feel dry, even when you've been dribbling into it for the best part of an hour. Horrible word, 'dribbling'. Implies no control, physical or mental. I preferred the word 'leak'. You can fix a leak.

I wandered off to our downstairs loo. Then a few minutes later a voice broke into my concentration:

'You've been in their ages! What are you up to?'

I was still delusional:

'Getting love-pump out is quite easy June, cramming it all back in again takes time.'

'Yeah right B.D.'

If only. In reality I was trying to work out whether it was time to change my incontinence pad. The used pad was so dry I could only tell whether it needed replacing by comparing its weight with a fresh one straight out of the box. Then it was obvious. Clever material technology.

I couldn't worry about my sex life while this damp pad occupied my nether regions. It was no good having an erection like a tent-pole if you were plagued with a fragrance issue. My strong desire was, to use that urological expression, to be 'dry'. Only an incontinent person knows the value of continence and how **thoroughly miserable** it would be for this situation to be prolonged. There's nothing worse than your other half charting your course through the shopping centre by following the scent of 'eau de ammonia'.
If you were drinking loads to keep the catheter happy, it will be awfully tempting to drink less in order to keep the incontinence pad happy. Don't. Water is essential to life. Along with beer of course.

Thankfully the incontinence issue improved fairly rapidly, and with it came increasing levels of confidence. Within a few days I was dry throughout the night. Within a week I was dry standing up. They were like mileposts along the road to recovery. I was grateful for this. The novelty of a day out accompanied by a bag full of heavy smelly used pads would not have lasted long, even allowing for the attention I'd get from inquisitive dogs.

I had been so focussed on the erectile dysfunction issue that I didn't give incontinence the pre-eminence it deserved. I lost sight of my priorities.
I thought back to when I was an apprentice, enjoying all those hypothetical drunken debates I took part in around the campfire. Would you rather be deaf or blind? Shag less or live longer? Now there was a new one we'd never even thought of: firmness or dryness? I was dry, but not yet firm. I'd settle for that.

After a few weeks I could cough, even sneeze, without leakage. Then my last Fragmin injection. Handing my box of 'sharps' into my local pharmacist felt like the end of a long journey. I started running again. At first a damp patch spread embarrassingly on the front of my shorts. To preserve my dignity, I'd drop to the floor and fiddle with my laces if a pedestrian or car came towards me. I avoided busy times otherwise I'd be bouncing up and down like a jack-in-the-box. If I was out in the rain, I'd wet my hands on the grass and then wipe them on my shorts to get them wet all over. Within a month, even this was dispensed with. I was watertight. I could even pass the ultimate test. The gold medal of continence: dry while passing wind with a full bladder.

A package had been left by the front door. Another discrete brown box with 'medical products' stamped on it. I opened the box. Some 'Attends' surgical underwear and incontinence pads. All my Christmases rolled into one. There was also a 'man bag' with the manufacturers logo discretely applied in one corner. It was helpfully designed to enable you to carry supplies of medical products about with you in a fashionable way. However, there was no way I was going to go into my local Wetherspoons with one of these slung casually over my shoulder. At least not in this instant internet age. A moment's Googling would reveal that my designer logo was in fact the brand name of a supplier of incontinence pads.

I had a follow-up phone call from the medical products company that had sent me my incontinence pads. Blimey, if I wanted to speak to Kate she was always too busy to pick up the phone, but the medical company always had time to give me a call:
'How are you Mr Meredith? I hope you're feeling well.'

I would accept sympathy from any quarter. Flattery as well. Not so bothered about sincerity anymore -these days it was flattery all the way. Especially now the future was a little brighter.

I pause for a moment, and realise that for anyone who is ***really*** ill, a compliment, however well meant, has to be anchored in reality. If you look, and feel, like death warmed up then being told you look good isn't going to convince anyone.

Somebody recently told me how much better I was looking, now my bone scan result was behind me. I thought I was doing really well, but the strain must have been showing.

I'd recently made the acquaintance of a woman who was undergoing chemotherapy after a major operation. She was remarkably positive and determined. One week she was bald, the next she's sporting a full head of 'hair'. Whichever option she chooses, her smile is always ready. She really was looking good and I don't hesitate to tell her.

'Mr Meredith?'
'Sorry, I was miles away. I'm fine thanks.
'Have you got everything you need?'
'Yes thanks'
'Well be sure to let us know in plenty of time if you need further supplies.'
'Ok'
'Is there anything else I can do for you while I'm on the phone?'
'Are you any good at fragmin injections?'

I came up behind June in the bathroom. My hands rested on her hips. I whispered in her ear:
'I've got something to show you!'

Then I turned, opened up my dressing gown, and blasted the back of the toilet bowl at full power.

It was like going back thirty years. I was like a child with a new toy.

'Look at this June!'

There was a groan of disappointment.

'Uh. I thought you meant...'

This was progress. The other...well...that might take a little time.

10 All is revealed

For the first time in almost 6 months, I was urinating naturally. No plastic tubes.

Rather than a short dribble, I was almost back to a full-power jet-wash. It was the only really impressive feature left now that I was a few cards short of a full deck.

I was even flushing undesirable debris down into the toilet bowl. Something I hadn't done for ages. I even sent a housefly down for a swim.

I was urinating well. My wonder-weapon may have lacked a bit of wonder, but I was feeling good.

June had just come back from a visit to Tracy, her hairdresser.
'You know my friend Tracy? The one who knows everything?'
'Yes.'
Tracy worked from home. She was a good listener, and in the course of dealing with her various clients, many juicy snippets of gossip came her way. It was like the gossip equivalent of a stock exchange. She got to know every bit of business, private or otherwise, that went on in the district. To the point that if there was any trouble in town, the first thing the police did was send a plain-clothes WPC round for some highlights.

'She told me your dentist is off work with cancer.'
I told June what she said to me as I left her surgery, just a few weeks ago.
'Blimey. Never mind about you. She must have been going through a difficult time herself.'
I remembered how nice it had been to receive cards when I was ill. I popped out and purchased a 'get well' card.
June saw me writing in it.

All is revealed

'Let's have a look.'
If anyone was capable of saying or doing the wrong thing at the wrong time it was me. I needed a second opinion. She held the card up:

'Dear Imogen. Sorry to hear you are unwell. Get well soon. I look forward to the day you are back at work, drilling into my teeth once again.
Regards.
David Meredith. One of your patients'

'Christ' she smiled 'bloody typical!'
In approval terms that was the equivalent of a standing ovation with bouquets landing at my feet.

I popped into my dentist, and handed over my card to the girl on reception.
'I'll see she gets it. There's been so many cards that we're having to pop round to her every Monday with the latest bundle.'
'Oh, um...that's really lovely.'
I paused for a moment.
'Do you mind,..do you mind if I ask how she is?'
'Well she's undergoing chemotherapy at the moment, but she's really positive. She's already started to accept appointments for a few months time.'
'That's good to hear.'
I remembered I had another appointment soon.
'Can I postpone my appointment for a few months? I'm not experiencing any pain so I'm sure I can delay it until she gets back.'
'Are you sure? That would really help. The other dentists are having to pick up her appointments.'

'No that's fine.'
I smiled at the receptionist and was on my way.

I had an appointment with 'The Whirlwind' -my surgeon. If past experience was anything to go by it would be conducted at break neck speed. It was best to have your questions ready before you went in -you might only have time for one. Here was the only man who knew my prostate better than I did. He'd spent literally hours looking at it. In a professional capacity of course. I don't know about your experience dear reader, but I always found it ***incredibly hard*** to concentrate on what was being said. Like my mind didn't really want to engage.

This post-operative meeting could only be conducted a little time after the operation, because he had to wait for the results from the laboratory. Here my prostate would be sectioned to give a picture of how extensive the cancer had been. Thankfully there were no pictures on the screen this time. I was happy to take his word for it:

'There was quite a bit of cancer.'

I felt my decision to opt for surgery had been vindicated. I took his words to mean that they had found more cancer than they were expecting. It was like a coded message. What he might have been saying was that it couldn't have been left any longer.

'We were able to spare your nerves on the one side, but on the other side the cancer was breaking through and we needed a margin of safety. Your seminal vesicles have been removed as well. Standard procedure.

We are going to prescribe some Cialis to improve blood flow to the penis, but it can take up to twelve months for your erectile dysfunction to improve. You will be required to perform a PSA test every three months to monitor your PSA level. Any questions?'

I'd recently been back into hospital for an ultrasound scan on my liver. This had been prompted by my poor liver function during my re-admission. It was on my mind.
'Is my liver function ok?'
'Oh….yes..all fine' he smiled.
They seemed reluctant to dwell on anything associated with my re-admission to hospital. It was as if we were going to get into a discussion about responsibility and blame, and we all knew where that might end up. I didn't want to go there.

I don't take work too seriously now. I don't really want to be there if I'm honest, but needs must. The other reason I still worked was pure self-interest. I felt safer. Mortality rates for people who retired were alarmingly high.
Cancer gives me a new perspective and I'm determined to enjoy every day. It doesn't matter what the level of urgency is: 'Frantic', 'Breathing optional' or 'Stimulants' -it makes no difference. I have a new mantra: 'A smile a day makes the deadline go away'. Although I resist the temptation to post such a thing in the conference room, or 'Mission Control' as I have begun to call it.

Thanks to cancer, and my closeness to retirement, I'm now free of the need to be 'on message' and can forget career considerations like status, jostling for position and wanting to have the final say at meetings. With all that gone, I almost **demand** not to be taken seriously. It's a kind of new-found recklessness that I thought I'd abandoned in my youth. Everyone feels the benefit of my new-found mellowness and understanding. I'm determined to show everyone what a nice person I am and how badly misunderstood I have been all these years. Like Bill Murray at the end of Groundhog Day, I exude calm enlightenment. And, in case I fall off my pedestal, that nice lady in HR will ensure there are no consequences for my actions.

Well not quite. I'm in the real world here, not Punxsutawney, and I still respond -if I think it will make a difference. I just don't lose any sleep over it. I'm rushing less, -noticing more.

I have a little nodding statue of Michaelangelo's 'David' on my desk. A little tap on the head from my forefinger, and it will immediately provide nodding re-assurance if things get difficult. Next to it stands my Rounders Umpiring certificate. This was the subject of much mirth among my colleagues. I had the last laugh however when I pointed out that each time I officiated, I had eighteen women under my command.

My Linkedin account is not the earnest, striving, dynamic and upwardly mobile place it used to be. I was once quite careful about who I allowed to join my professional network. Unless they could be of value in progressing my 'career' they were just ignored, their request finally rejected with a pile of others when I had to do a bit of housekeeping. Nowadays, my standards have dropped a bit. I've lowered the entry bar. My employment history means I get a lot of requests from female sales reps from Korean electronics companies. At one time these would have been rejected out of hand, but now, if they are good looking, they're waved on in. I'm sorry Melon Dong of Longthong Circuits in Seoul that I rejected your request last year. If you request again now, you'll find you'll be granted access to my formerly exclusive little club.

I was at work, waving a doughnut in front of Glenn again -trying to bend him to my will. He was trying to make sense of the latest corporate communication from Carson in Michigan, probing for hidden meaning and profound insight:
'Investing more than the competition ties to our segment's value proposition to grow the top line faster than our industry peers.'[*]

In his previous communication, he'd stated his desire to tour the various parts of the merged organisation looking for 'synergy'. This had caused a panic as various members of the hierarchy desperately scoured the premises looking for some in advance of his visit. I'd done what I could -looked under my desk, but without success.

We wondered what it was like to be Carson, starting a high-tech empire from within a pile of fast-food cartons in a trailer park in down-town Michigan. Some minion peeling away his stale tracksuit bottoms in readiness for a news conference. We imagined Carson clearing his throat, ready to impart some pearl of wisdom, while pilgrims from all over the galaxy gathered at his feet, ready to assemble the spewing words into some semblance of order.

I wanted to move that address line back again but my doughnut bribe wasn't having the desired effect. He announced he was on a diet and I was getting part of the blame. I waved it under his nose again but his resolve was strong. He stood up, palm on chest and looked upwards:
'My body is a temple!'
I was there in a flash:
'But nobody worships there!'

---

[*] actual quote

It was part of the verbal sparring necessary when the pressure was on, but as we enjoyed the joke, I suffered a pang of loss. My quip was a more accurate reflection of *my* current predicament, not his.

I'm getting even more sympathetic glances than usual these days so I'm sure colleagues know about my illness. A woman, who I don't know particularly well, passed behind by my desk. She looked a bit pre-occupied, but as she approached we exchanged smiles, and as her shadow passed across my screen I felt a touch on the shoulder. I knew the moment she was gone that I would never forget her unspoken gesture. We'd only ever discussed work-related matters, but in that moment she made me feel my burden wasn't mine alone.

The unspoken gestures are always the best. The receiver gets to interpret them in their own way. Of course, at my age I might just be reading the signs wrong, the touch might mean they've tripped on the carpet, and the sympathetic glance probably means I've got mixed shoes on again.

I also find I'm a little bit forgetful now. On a recent holiday to Spain we were driving to a local town. We were an hour into our trip. The sun had climbed up into a clear blue sky and it was getting warm in the car. So warm, that I needed to stop and remove my coat. My big chunky twenty year-old SLR camera was down by my feet. The theory was that I would be able to get to it quickly if something interesting turned up, but I could feel it getting in the way. It was annoying me. I pulled over. Out came the camera, and I put it down somewhere while I removed my coat. This was then chucked into the back of the car. Then we were off again.

All is revealed

Soon I spotted a police car waiting near a roundabout. Nice car. An Alfa with all the lights and stripes. They made eye contact with me as I went by. One of them pointed, but I was out of there. Shortly afterwards the police car was behind me. Despite my slow driving, it made no attempt to overtake. It followed me as I turned into a side street. I was on my best behaviour now -I even remembered to indicate. There was an old lady on the side of the road. I slowed to let her cross but she seemed a little reluctant.
'I'm not sure she really wants to go Dave.'
Never mind. I forced her across the road with wild arm gyrations. This must surely have counted in my favour. Then, as we passed through some traffic lights, I slowed, even though they were green. Another bonus point, but unfortunately his flashing blue lights finally made an appearance. I'd been stopped.

I got out of the car. He spoke to me in Spanish. Keen to show off my language skills (and be sophisticated in front of June), I replied in broken French. June gazed up at me with new-found ardour.
He shook his head 'Inglesi?'
All sorts of things went through my head as I stood there on the pavement:
Was I speeding? Did I miss a signal? Did I have my Rick Astley CD up too loud?

I couldn't understand much of what he was saying, but I'm sure I heard the word 'camera'. My heart sank. I was going to be charged with speeding.
'I told you to slow down!' came a helpful voice from inside the car. Then he seemed to want to see my camera. His hands were up around his eyes, like he was taking a picture. I was really puzzled by now. I was looking around inside the car for the camera, but I

couldn't find it. Like most of my possessions, it was a bit of a relic. It wasn't there. I've been asked to produce a passport before but never a camera.

I faced the officer and shrugged. Then I noticed his colleague heading towards me with what looked astonishingly like my chunky old SLR camera. I was flummoxed.

The officer patted the roof of my car and made a falling motion with his hands.

They were both laughing by now. I was all thanks but still confused by their sleight of hand.

Only later did I realise that after I threw my coat in the back of the car, I must have driven away with the camera on the roof. It must have rolled off as I sped past them on the roundabout!

Life was getting back to normal. I hadn't been to skittles for a while, but now that I was feeling better I decided I should honour them with my presence. As I opened the door of the skittle alley, they all turned and clapped. So they should. Prostate cancer affects one man in eight. After a quick head count, I concluded that I'd taken one for the team.

The Doll's House was finished. It had done its job of stopping me worrying. It had given me something to focus on. It was time to hand it over to someone who would really look after it -my granddaughter. She was eight. Just about the right age for this level of responsibility. I used to take her litter picking when she was more pliable. I'd kit her out in a high-visibility jacket, and one of those robot arms to pick the litter up with. We'd sweep the high street for rubbish and provided she filled a bag, she was given the freedom of our local 'Thorntons' shop. She was much more sophisticated now -not so easily persuaded to indulge grandad in one of his silly escapades.

My daughter and her family were round for tea. My granddaughter was allowed to 'discover' the doll's house in the conservatory. She came rushing in and dragged her mum off to have a look. I heard my daughter's voice fading away down the hallway:
'What do you mean 'come and see our house? It's miles away!'
Everything went quiet for ten minutes. Then I went out to have a look. There they both were, opening the doors and switching the lights on and off.
My granddaughter gave me a hopeful look, trying to stake first claim ahead of her mother:
'Who's it for Granddad?'
Well, what was I supposed to say to that?
'Give me a hug and it's yours. I've brushed my teeth and I've got deodorant on – it doesn't get much better than this!'

It was time to thank a few people, particularly the medical staff. They had just saved my life. What price did I put on that? Maybe I could just phone up the urology ward receptionist, and ask her to pass on my thanks. Perhaps I could see if they had a Facebook page and give them that most empty of gestures - a 'like'. Maybe a card? These didn't seem adequate, but what would? I couldn't just shrug my shoulders and move on. I thought back to my daughter's 'Thorntons' delivery to my place of work. I went through my medical folder. I made a note of everyone who had played a part in my treatment.
My surgeon, the nurses, even the woman who cleaned the ward with such good humour. She claimed to have dusted me off on one occasion when she discovered me asleep on her round. Fifteen

individually named boxes of luxury chocolates. All done on-line. 'Thorntons' -you did me proud! I sign off the accompanying card with the words:
'Don't take this the wrong way, but I hope I never see any of you ever again (or at least not for a long while)'

I did think of a charity fundraiser for the hospital. I could join June on one of her shopping expeditions and rattle a collection tin. What could possibly go wrong? I already had my opening gambit:
'£1 to see my scars. £2 not to see them.'
Probably better than:
'I'm collecting for impoverished husbands'

I wanted to thank June so I took her into town. Minus the collection tin. We paused outside a jewellers. I suppose with my newfound mindfulness and philosophical bent, I was now more relaxed about money. Indeed I was -but not **this** relaxed. My shopping was like an SAS military mission, carried out with precision and the minimum of civilian casualties. June shopped with a different vocabulary. She didn't 'want' a new handbag, she 'needed' one. She didn't 'buy' a new telly, she 'invested' in one. I had so much still to learn. Why you need a 60inch high-definition entertainment system to watch 'Cash in the Attic' was never properly explained to me. 'Need to know' etc. Anyway, I digress. I did my best to walk past the sparkly window but I was suddenly overcome by an overwhelming feeling of loneliness. I had no option but to head back into the jewellers to see where June had got to.
It's time to break marital confidentiality again and reveal that I wasn't the only person with an illness in this relationship.
June had a longstanding medical condition. She had a skin complaint which mainly affected her neck, wrists and fingers. She

suffered from terrible skin rashes if these areas of her body came into contact with base metals. Hers was a particularly bad case, because the rashes would spontaneously erupt, not just on contact with base metals, but any metal -apart from gold and platinum -or so she said.

Not that anyone's ever actually witnessed it of course.

Unusually, she seemed reluctant to bother the doctor with her problem. She bore her illness stoically and without complaint. Like many other women, apparently.

11. What was it like for you darling?

There's no hiding the fact that a prostatectomy will seriously damage your sex life. It's a testament to the dedication of the medical staff that they make quite an effort to help you make the most of what's left. They are almost apologetic about having curtailed your 'nocturnal activities'. Well there's no need to apologise. You saved my life. Instead of a 'managed' exit, my unknown destiny has been re-instated. Once again, I have the normal uncertainty of not knowing the 'when' or the 'how'.
There's no doubt that as a man I feel slightly diminished. Not quite complete. An enjoyable and essential part of who I am is no longer there. I'm still a man in other respects: I don't like shopping. I probably watch too much football. And I'm often not listening when June is talking, (but privately, I excuse myself on the basis that a woman's capacity to talk exceeds a man's ability to listen). Anyway -these were survival mechanisms.
It's a small price to pay and I have absolutely no regrets.

I have sadly accepted that my sex life is over in the normal sense. I am no longer a threat to women. Somebody told me I should live every day like it was my last. Superficially this was good advice, but if I acted upon it the lawn would be a foot high and that shelf would never get put up. Of course, I understand the sentiment. I still have my memories of when I was 'The Stud' and women made impossible demands of me.
If only.
It's still possible to be intimate, but now you experience what is known in the trade as a 'dry orgasm'. Still pleasurable, but without the intensity you experienced when all your important little places were still joined up. If you're looking for positives then at least

there is no longer a trip to the bathroom after it's all over. It's much neater and tidier. Oh, and you can have as many 'dry orgasms' as you like.

It was a warm spring night. The birds were in song. Sap was beginning to rise. It was the time of year when a man's thoughts turned to love. Everything was starting to grow -well **nearly** everything. Someone was refusing to co-operate, but this time I was going to get lucky. Me and wonder-weapon were going to be reconciled. He was going to get a wake-up call. I'd engaged the services of a mediator -a little blue tablet. I was so confident that I rinsed with mouthwash. I even splashed on a bit of expensive after-shave my son had discarded when he left home fifteen years ago. I'd even been busy with the deodorant.

I stood in the middle of the living room in a dressing gown, with my Viagra tablet in one hand and a glass of water in the other. There was a table nearby where the glass could be abandoned if things got out of control. I did think about a count-down but that might be tempting fate.

I told June not to come too close. Anything could happen. I didn't want any health and safety issues.

I checked my surroundings. Made sure I had plenty of headroom. Plenty of space. I didn't want to turn around suddenly and sweep all the ornaments off the mantlepiece. I'd read that the erection could last for four hours so I cleared my diary. I told June to have a little light reading handy. There would be no problem with premature ejaculation this time. Probably the opposite. I wouldn't be sure when to stop. I could keep going for as long as my stamina would allow. I was eager to please.

This was a new situation though. We couldn't just slip into our old routines. We would have to establish a whole new range of protocols. Would I have that fabled dry orgasm? Maybe now we'd

both have to fake an orgasm. We'd have to improvise. Then she'd have to indicate to me when the earth had been sufficiently moved for her. Maybe she could ring a little bell. If I was too enthusiastic maybe she'd resort to smothering my face with a cloth soaked in chloroform. Possibly play an episode of Gardner's Question Time on-demand using Radio 4 I-player, or whatever they call it. You can't plan these things.
The tablet was on my lips. Then with one mouthful of water it was down my throat. I'll resist the stiff neck joke.

Nothing.

June tried some encouragement. I made light of the lack of progress:
'Careful, you might unleash forces beyond your control.'
She gave a shrug:
'Doesn't look like it B.D.'
There was no sign of life. I joke about it now, but it was pretty disappointing. Viagra had been the ace up my sleeve. It was going to require a bit more than a tablet.

The hospital offered me a follow-up appointment where potential solutions to the erectile dysfunction problem could be discussed. These consisted of tablets, injections and vacuum pumps. I probably don't need to explain the first two. The third consists of a tube with a little hand-held vacuum pump. This was placed over the penis and the tube was then evacuated with the pump. Then ...well do I need to explain further? 'Nature fills a vacuum', or at least that's what they told me at school. My curiosity was aroused. There was scope to get a little carried away here but my investigations revealed that what worked in theory couldn't always be relied upon in practice.

I could imagine a situation when the planets were aligned, Cheltenham Town had just won the FA Cup, and we were both 'in the mood' at exactly the same time. I'd then spend twenty minutes in the bathroom with injections or the vacuum device, only to return and find that June had fallen asleep. It was clearly not ideal. I did think of commissioning a promotional video for June to watch, while she waited for wonder-weapon to be readied for action. You know the kind of thing: Muscled stud kissing a woman tenderly in a plunge pool under a waterfall. I'd probably get Brad Pitt to play my role. I needed to manage expectations so I'd make sure all the lights were extinguished before I made my entrance. There was no doubt that from now on, sex was going to be a challenge. We had always managed without 'equipment' up until now. Ok I confess, maybe a crane and harness to raise and lower me into position. And possibly in my younger days, a little springboard at the foot of the bed.

Later I discussed these options with my brother in law. He had no luck with the tablets or the vacuum pump, but had enjoyed some initial success with the injections. An injection on each side of the penis was enough to get you off the starting line. The problem was the result wasn't consistent along the whole length of the penis. Sometimes it would bend one way before straightening up again. He joked that he almost went out into the garden on one occasion to get a bit of bamboo cane. Of course, if Venus has aligned with Mars solely for your benefit, then it's possible to get a little impatient. He tried an injection on each side but the response had been a little slow. He then injected even more. He ended up with a greatly enlarged penis and a problem that could only be resolved with a visit to A&E. There he sat in considerable pain while the hospital was scoured for someone with the experience required to treat this problem. I will spare you the details on this occasion. Suffice to say the whole experience was distressing enough for him to abandon any further efforts. I was already inclined not to experiment, so after speaking to my brother in law I decided not to take up the offer of help.

Don't be discouraged. Although it didn't work for him, it doesn't necessarily mean it won't work for you. Everyone's experience will be different. It's all a question of how important a sex life is to you. Of course, the removal of your seminal vesicles will mean no semen, so lubrication will be in short supply. So if you've decided to give penis-pumps and injections a go, you might also want to add lubricating gel to your toy cupboard.

Of course, there was the ultimate solution: a procedure known as a strapadictomy. This was something you might joke about with your friends in the pub. They must surely exist but I'd never seen a real one. Maybe it was advertised in the magazine I'd seen in hospital – next to hearing aids. I was pretty sure June wouldn't be interested. In any case -where would you keep it? If you took it on holiday, you would have to be quite sure you didn't leave it behind. I didn't want a phallus-shaped parcel arriving from a cruise company. Anyway -they probably didn't have one in my size.

The plain fact is, at least in my experience, you won't be able to get an erection **on demand**.
However, post operation, you'll be pleasantly surprised to wake up in the middle of the night to find an erection you could hang a towel

on. The problem is, by the time you've woken up your other half and got the mood music going, it's already gone into hiding. Like a child that's been caught with its hand in the sweetie jar. The most surprising thing is that wonder-weapon is **perfectly capable** of getting into the operating position without assistance of any kind, but it plays hide and seek. Coyly showing you what might have been if you hadn't so brutally let it down.

Most of the time it's bashful and shy, but when it does its private showing, you'll throw the duvet off, turn the light on, and marvel at this magic trick of nature. How did I ever take this for granted? It was so **incredibly empowering**. How could you possibly explain this feeling to a woman? A debit card with infinite credit wouldn't even get close. What other part of the anatomy makes a transformation like this? When it inevitably disappears back into its shell again after a minute or so, you'll get sad and sentimental at what you've lost.

I was now prepared to forgive wonder-weapon for all those indiscrete moments when he unpredictably took the initiative on my behalf, sometimes with embarrassing results. Those moments of insubordination. For most of the time Love-Pump, you've been a friend I could rely on. We were such a good team, weren't we? Until I ignored your feelings. Please forgive me, and come back to me some day. I will be your Jack again, if you will be my beanstalk. Anyway, I know I let you down badly wonder-weapon, but if you ever come back to me I promise never to take you for granted ever ever **ever** again.

We've had to adapt. Although the train doesn't enter the tunnel anymore, a lot more time is now spent cleaning the engine.
I did consider going into business, manufacturing penis-pumps. What could possibly go wrong? It wouldn't have to **actually** work.

After all, how many people are going to take it back for a refund? Can you imagine yourself at the counter of Boots with a queue behind you, while a young female shop assistant shows you where you're going wrong?

Another visit to the dentist, and I'm waiting at the reception desk. I'd had so much time off work recently that I made an appointment outside work hours. I was probably the last appointment of the day. The woman in front of me obviously lived in one of the outlying villages. She was complaining about the bell-ringers:
'They went on for an hour this morning. Flippin' racket.'
I caught the eye of the receptionist. She forced a smile. We were both thinking the same thing. Then the woman finally retired to a seat -no doubt relieved at being able to unburden herself of one of life's great difficulties. Then it was my turn. The receptionist's fingers flashed over the keyboard.
'Take a seat Mr Meredith.'
Soon enough, an assistant ventured into the waiting room:
'Mr Meredith?'
Then it was my turn in the familiar chair. Not my usual dentist this time. A bit odd. Anyway, we made small talk, but as always I was pre-occupied with what was coming next. I knew he'd be scraping away at my teeth soon enough. Getting under my fillings, probing for weaknesses and peeling back my gums. Unusually, he started by taking an inventory. This wouldn't take long. Quite a few had already left for pastures new:
'7 Amalgam, 6 Absent, 5 absent, 4 composite..' and so it went on. Very few passed without comment.
'All good Mr Meredith. I'll see you again in six months' time.'
I was so relieved at avoiding the drill, that the significance of his remark escaped me.

Then I was at the desk handing over my notes. The waiting room was empty. The receptionist handed me an appointment ticket. They were closing for another day.
'There you are Mr Meredith'
'Thanks.'
I paused for a moment.
'Um, it's nothing personal, but can I see Imogen next time?'
She tried to say something, but could only look anxiously at her colleague:
'Were you aware she....'
'Yes. She was having chemo. I dropped a card in a few months ago.'
The colour drained from her face.
'Sorry Mr Meredith..' she replied with a breaking voice:
'Imogen isn't going to make it.'

12. Looking forwards

Cancer changes you. Some of us work less, play more, try to make up for lost time. Some of us pull friends and family closer; some push them away. I don't want to be at work anymore but needs must. I try and get the most out of every day, whoever I'm with, whatever I'm doing. I'm talking less. Listening more.
When I'm browsing the internet forums and read stories of men who have not had it so good, I have twinges of guilt. Especially when they reveal that it was discovered too late. Among them are people like me, who still need to earn a living. Then I think of all those retirement plans that came to nought. The impact on loved ones. The grandchildren to whom they will be but a vague memory. It's too awful to dwell on and there's nothing I can say to make it better. The truth is that none of us really knows what's around the next bend, be it a car crash or a cancer recurrence, and an almost universal outcome of this disease is a more mindful approach to the time that remains. We only get a temporary reprieve. You might jump one hurdle, but none of us knows when the next hurdle will appear, and how high it might be.

Like many other profound events in life, cancer is an experience that takes and gives. It has taken an essential part of me away, but it has also given. It's shown me that I am not alone. That I am appreciated and loved. It's taught me the value of time, and that I cannot waste it, or allow someone else to steal it away from me. It's given me a better understanding, not only of who I am, but what *I still* could be -even in the time that remains. It's taught me the value of anonymous acts of kindness, not just with family - that's a given- but even with strangers -*especially* with strangers.

Cancer leaves its marks, even if you can't see and describe them with precision.

I will say that one of the best decisions I made along the way was to be as open as I possibly could with my friends, family and work colleagues. Fear and anxiety thrive in cold, dark, lonely places and by inviting others along on my journey, I had warmth, light and companionship. Of course, not everyone wants to know, especially work colleagues. Most people will not want your illness to be an added complication in their working hours, and you should respect that. You don't want people diving into a broom cupboard when they see you walking down the corridor itching to talk about your latest catheter. The world of work is tough enough already.

There is life after cancer. Granted, it may not be the life you expected, but it's still possible to make plans and tick a few things off that bucket list. Here's a couple of statistics that you may already be aware of:
One in eight men get Prostate Cancer. One in three people will get some kind of cancer in their lifetime.
Of course, having contracted cancer once, there is always the anxiety that it will come back at some point. Especially when you have already beaten odds of eight to one against. This is an understandable worry, but there is really nothing to be gained by it and you shouldn't allow it to spoil the days that lie ahead. Don't let your uncertain future stop you from enjoying this wonderful present. Easy to say I know.
You're bound to feel slightly cheated. To ask 'why me?'
Unfortunately, in life, there are no guarantees. Especially when you have entered the age of uncertainty. We need to remind ourselves that being old is better than the other alternative.

You're going to be tempted to look at survival rates. The difficulty with a five-year survival rate for example, is that by definition, it's working on data that is at least five years old. They will present a gloomier picture than is actually the case, given that better treatments and earlier detection techniques are improving outcomes all the time. Now I'm not burying my head in the sand, but being a statistic myself, I prefer to focus on enjoying the time I have left. Five years hence, I don't want to be anxiously looking at my watch.
I'm quite happy to talk about survival rates, but unless you've found a stat that says a high beer, chocolate and exercise regime has been shown to improve outcomes, then I don't spend too much time worrying about them. I have reverted back to type with my 'ignorance is bliss' approach. Anyway, I'm aiming to be part of those better statistics that will hopefully be published sometime in the future.

It's also tempting to look back on whether any aspects of your diet or lifestyle could have contributed to your cancer. There's a lot of information out there and no doubt these things are worth exploring. I'm quite happy to sip 'Essence of Rhinoceros Toenail' if it will make any difference, but while the evidence for dietary change is quite compelling, it isn't conclusive. I focus on being kind to my body, and knowing my limitations. Of course, it's never too late to make changes, but with my family history and lifetime fondness for chocolate, I feel the die is cast to a certain extent.
My diet, even post cancer, isn't going to win any awards, but I've reduced my cholesterol level from 6.3 to 5.6 by switching to a cholesterol lowering spread. This isn't a clinical trial obviously, but

it seems to show that it is possible to affect some general improvement in health without living like a hermit.

To conclude, I've been through this cancer thing relatively easily. I have had some dark moments, but I have always been positive. Luck has a lot to do with the result, but a positive attitude will pull you through whatever your prognosis. Heed the advice you are given. During the time you have your catheter drink as much as you can. Then drink some more. Make sure you do your pelvic floor exercises. The harder you work at them -the luckier you will be.
Post cancer, there's a time to be reflective. A time to change things -make those dreams come true. Maybe you want to work less, play more. If you're in this situation and want to make changes, now's your opportunity. There will never be a better time to have your ideas accepted.

We were out with Anne and John. There was the usual banter. He would tease me about my support for Cheltenham Town. I would get my revenge at some point. If I found myself next to him at the urinal, I'd express surprise that he could stand so close.
They knew I had spoken to 'Sandy Coloured Products' to see if I could shorten my working week. They asked how things were going.
'Dave doesn't work Monday's now' said June.
'I don't work Tuesday's either but I go in!'
'Dave...' -she threw a glance at John, '..we're….we're really glad that it all worked out for you. For both of you.'
It caught me by surprise. I didn't know what to say. June came to my rescue:
'Thanks Anne.'

It was one of the nicest things a woman had ever said to me. It was right up there with what June said to me once when we were trying to buy her a dress for a wedding. We were in a really exclusive shop, and she had fallen in love with the most expensive dress in there. There was a groan of disappointment, and the offending item was returned to the rail:
'They haven't got it in my size'.

John returned with four glasses of bubbly. This really was an extraordinary act of extravagance on his part, and I was privileged to have lived long enough to see it. We mentioned the cottage but it clashed with a wedding they had been invited to. It looked like we were going to be on our own.

I'm continuing with the running. I started running in my twenties, and not because I enjoyed it. I rationalised the effort and pain by promising myself it would extend my health and fitness into old age. Make me immune from the illnesses that plagued everyone else. Of course, it must help, but it hasn't worked out quite as I planned. Maybe it's just a delusion. A delusion that exaggerates our place in the world and our impact upon it, telling us we are more significant than we really are and that we're in charge of things that will always be beyond our control.
It's the voice that says if we prepare, practice, do everything just right, everything will be Ok
So much for that idea.
Now, I continue to run because I can release those endorphins and enjoy the feeling of mild euphoria that takes over once I've finished. It's a feeling that lasts for the rest of the day. It's prescription free, and it helps me banish those anxious thoughts.

I'm doing my regular Sunday morning run, and I've turned out of a country lane onto a busy road. I'm aware of a few people standing around. Some lean over their front gates. Others collect in small groups at junctions and lay-bys. They are all looking in my direction. The nearest people start to clap. I glance down -I'm 'dry' -it really isn't such a big deal -honest.

'Come on -keep going' they shout.

I'm confused, but touched by their support. I assume June has passed on the good news about my recovery to her hairdresser. I'm puzzled though -even that wouldn't explain this level of interest.

By now my chest is out and I'm taking big strides. I'm doing my Roger Bannister impression, my head tilted slightly backwards in mock agony.

In the distance there's a high-viz jacket and some cones. I'm straight though a puddle and a lay-by breaks out in spontaneous applause.

Just at the point I think I'm going to wake up, another runner overtakes me. Our eyes meet.

'Alright mate?' I venture in a workman-like tone.

No response. He's already pulling away from me when I spot his competitor number. I look behind. Even more numbers. I've gate-crashed my local half marathon and I've never led the field before. I bail out into a side-street before I collapse in a breathless heap.

Cancer changes things. You're entitled to spend a bit more time doing those things that make life a little better. At least, that's what I tell myself as I struggle to get my breath back.

It was purely by chance that I didn't die of prostate cancer like my father and grandfather. If the cancer hadn't caused a narrowing of the urethra and consequent chronic retention, I would have been completely unaware of it. It was only because the chronic retention led in turn to a urinary tract infection, that it was even suspected. The lesson here chaps is to get yourself checked out. Don't leave it to chance. Women are much better at looking after themselves than we are. Much more willing to go and see their doctor. We men need to be more proactive -to look after ourselves.

Let's stop being so fatalistic about our health. Just imagine for a moment that your local NHS has been split into a men's hospital and a women's hospital.
In the women's hospital there are patients in the corridors, no medicines left and staff are taking stimulants in order to keep going. Other staff are being signed off with work-related stress. The woman's hospital even has its own motorway junction. The government complain that they can't afford to run it.
In the men's hospital, by contrast, a cleaner walks past shelves of unused medicines before popping into the operating theatre to give it the occasional dust-over. The staff sit around playing cards, pausing occasionally to sign death certificates. It can be found in a small unit on an industrial estate. Hardly anyone knows where it is. It runs at a profit.

OK. A bit absurd I must admit, but June knows a woman who goes along to her local GP when her relationship isn't going too well. Personally, I feel this is a waste of the GP's precious time, but it does show how much more willing women are to seek help. This isn't any fault of the girls, rather that we boys need to get ourselves checked out and start taking our health seriously!

If you are experiencing problems passing urine, or you are passing urine more frequently, or there's some family history of Prostate

Cancer, then get yourself checked out. If you are over fifty years of age and have concerns, then discuss them with your GP.

Try and find out as much as you can about your family's medical history. Don't assume, like I did, that everything is on file. If your family has a history of Prostate Cancer, then do speak up. It's gambling with your health to do otherwise

Bear in mind that the PSA test by itself is not conclusive. It's possible to have cancer with a low PSA level. It's also possible for a high reading to be caused by a urinary tract infection, certain medications, prostate stimulation or exercise -particularly cycling. The PSA test should be used in conjunction with other diagnostic tools in order to build up a clear picture.

Differentiating between aggressive cancers and those that can safely be left alone is the current challenge facing the medical profession and one for which the PSA test, by itself, is an inadequate tool. So the PSA test is not perfect, but it's all we have at the moment.

The treatment timescales are uncomfortably long. The appointments with key people are too rushed. In this situation, an early diagnosis is essential. If you have any concerns then make that appointment -today.

The treatment is at times uncomfortable, and your dignity will take a bashing, but if you are thinking of getting yourself tested please don't be discouraged. It should be apparent to you by now that I am not a hero. If I can get through it -you can too. When your health is at risk you will be surprised at how strong you can be. Visit the Prostate Cancer UK website for more information. Be pro-active. Don't needlessly put yourself at risk. Your health is the most precious thing you have.

I was off work for four weeks and was watertight within three weeks (excluding jogging) so my recovery was swift. I put this down to my fitness and a Gymnastic Bronze in the Pelvic Floor routine. However, I suspect that the Da Vinci process played a big part in the recovery because the surgical incisions, while numerous, are all fairly small, allowing for faster healing. However, my erectile dis-function shows no sign of improving but **every case is different** and recovery times will vary. It's not unusual for incontinence to last for several months.

I just had my third PSA test. This showed a slight rise. Another rise in three months time will mean there was a small amount of cancer still remaining, which will have to be dealt with by radiotherapy. My surgeon re-assured me:
'Statistically Mr Meredith -you're going to die of old age.'
I guess I should have been slightly deflated. A medical professional has just confirmed that I'm not going to live forever after all, but I found his words strangely comforting.

Almost a year on from my operation my erectile dis-function shows no sign of getting better.
I was told it might take twelve months for it to improve. The anniversary of my operation is approaching and I did think about booking a weekend in a romantic getaway to celebrate, but that might be tempting fate. Knowing that I went into the operating theatre at 9am, I wouldn't want to spend our first morning away looking impatiently at my watch.
A woman reading this book may, or may not, be surprised to see the amount of attention given to erectile dysfunction, but then men and women have different priorities. This was brought home

to me recently when I read a book about breast cancer. The woman bravely endured a long course of chemotherapy after her operation, and while the discovery and treatment of her cancer occupied eight chapters, her hair-loss was given four chapters just by itself. Different priorities.

I'm walking along the coastal path to the old rectory at Rhosilli, loaded with luggage. The moon is sailing out to sea. It's dusk. I pause for a moment. A breeze carries the smell of kelp up onto the headland. I hear the distant crash of a wave and turn just in time to see its little white chargers. Then a hiss as the spume responds to the timeless pull of the moon.
I get a bit reflective for a moment. Thanks to cancer, I have a whole new perspective of what is important in life, I have discovered that I am loved (not unconditionally of course -I'm still making the life insurance payments) and I can once again jet-wash the toilet bowl.

As we approach the cottage, I notice there are a few lights on. I turn to June:
'Strange?'
'Maybe the cleaners left them on.'
The door is slightly ajar. I push it open, and drop my bags in the porch.
'Let's explore!'
I open the lounge door:
'Surprise! Surprise!'
A gaggle of people. My step-mother. My daughter and her family. Our friends Anne and John. There are hugs all round.
'I thought none of you could make it?'
The following morning, I'm sat at a picture window looking out to sea. My mind wanders back over forty years. A young lad and some

friends are playing in the surf with their canoes. Not a care in the world.

'I could murder a cup of tea.'

June startles me out of my thoughts. Her request is a sign to the others that I am better now and ought to be treated like a normal person. My comfortable period of indulgence is over. I remember my conversation with Kate.

My snail had won the race.

Postscript

'I've looked at your MRI scan and noticed a couple of spots on your pelvis'.

These words signalled that, a year after my prostatectomy, my battle with cancer wasn't quite finished. The oncology consultant was going off-script. He was supposed to tell me that my rising PSA level would require a course of radiotherapy. This would have been focussed on the space my prostate once occupied with the intention of killing those persistent remnants of my cancerous prostate.

My appointment had gone well up to this point, but then there was a pause and meaningful eye contact. A pause is unusual. Almost a luxury item. An extravagance when your appointment is the last one in the day and everyone's glancing at the clock. Its significance should not go unnoticed. It meant a deviation from the script -and so it proved. It heralded bad news.

He'd spoken in measured and considered tones. This had been quite encouraging -maybe I would have time to reflect on what he was telling me while the appointment was still taking place. This would be so much better than going home with your head swimming with unasked questions. Unfortunately this initial impression didn't last long. There was a clue immediately -he didn't even take the time to sit down, preferring to lean against a bed. I always had the impression with all my appointments that I was merely borrowing the specialist in front of me. He, or she, had always to be prepared to be scrambled at a moment's notice for an emergency elsewhere.

'Before I can approve the radiotherapy I need a second MRI scan which I can compare with your earlier scan to see if these spots have developed into anything. It's probably nothing to worry about. They might be bone spurs, harmless abnormalities or areas of dense bone.'

'Are you saying I've got cancer? My bone scan was clear!'
'It's just a precaution. The most important issue for you now is that the next course of treatment is relevant for your situation.'

When they stick to the script, these appointments are routine. When they unexpectedly veer off course, that giddying feeling of dread grips your stomach and you desperately want him to focus his attention on somebody else. The earlier scan he was referring to was associated with my Prostatectomy and was now about eighteen months old. He caught my anxious expression:

'I'm pretty confident there's nothing to worry about. I'll book the scan and also book the radiotherapy course to follow afterwards so we don't waste any time.'

I responded as calmly as I could:
'What if the spots have changed?'
'Then the treatment will be different.'

I looked round the little room. Bare magnolia walls, scuffed paintwork. A bed and a number of tired little chairs. The only object to break the monotony was a little notice board. It provided a home for some basic sign language instruction and a notice about returning medicines. This bleak little space was a perfect setting for an occasion such as this. The last thing you needed here was anything remotely optimistic.

This was all I needed. Another period of gut-wrenching worry. The enemy were supposed to be defeated. The radiotherapy was supposed to be a 'mopping up' operation. Joining the cancer club was beginning to sound like the lyrics to 'Hotel California' -one of the Eagles greatest hits:

'You can check out, but you can never leave.'

I would have had the radiotherapy there and then - just to be pro-active. However, thirty-three daily radiotherapy sessions were not to be treated lightly - especially if they were no longer appropriate. Especially if there were now too many targets. Especially if the suspect was a fugitive, now on the run.

Further questions could wait until after the MRI scan, but I was bound for another spell of knawing uncertainty. It was clear to me that my future now depended on how ambitious these spots decided to be. If the second MRI scan showed they'd become more prevalent or that they'd gone walkabout then we were going down a different road. We would be trying to hold cancer back, not get rid of it. He tried to re-assure me by showing me my bone scan report which showed no sign of the cancer having spread beyond the prostate. My next question could be postponed for now. Bone cancer was almost always a secondary cancer, so how could this be explained?

So there you are. Despite my finely crafted ending we have another chapter. You can't complain you're not getting value for money can you? If you are already persuaded to get yourself (or a loved one) checked out then read no further. If you are still undecided then read on. You'll get an insight into the perspective of an otherwise healthy individual whose life expectancy might be needlessly cut

Postscript

short. I had no desire to extend this book any further. Certainly no ideas about a sequel. Fame and fortune as a writer would be nice but a boring life from now on would probably have been better for all concerned. I didn't want to be a writer who suffered for his art.

As is the routine post-operation, your PSA level is monitored at three-monthly intervals. I already knew about the significance of the PSA reading post-operation. A small rise in PSA reading which levelled off was indicative of a remnant of healthy prostate tissue. This was nothing to worry about and would be monitored at regular intervals. However, a continued rise in PSA level would indicate that a small amount of cancer was still present. This would be persuaded to leave by the application of radiotherapy. My PSA reading continued to rise so the Urology department passed me on to the Oncology department like an unwanted present.

Of course, while you're battling cancer you are fully mobilised - mentally and physically. Once the battle has been won there follows a period of anxious reflection. Thoughts of mortality. Of course, none of us will be here forever and that isn't something that concerns me too much. It's the transition from here to there that sometimes bothers me a little, rather than the thought of not being here itself. Despite this, I'm pretty sure I'm not going to cope too well when the final curtain falls. I tell myself it's ok to be scared. Only when I read the obituary column in the local paper do I realise the significant difference between words like 'peaceful' and 'brave'.
It's then that I think of the Digital Rectal Examination and the discovery that the anticipation is often worse than the actual event. This is what I hope for when my tide finally goes out.

Postscript

Then I get angry that there is no screening programme for Prostate Cancer. We men are left to simply drift innocently along life's path with our fingers crossed. I'm angry that this could easily have been diagnosed earlier with a cautionary test. I'm angry that I'm having to deal with all this while I still need to earn a living. I'm angry that there's no mechanism for testing those with a family history of Prostate Cancer. Anger is a waste of energy now.

I'm looking at my financial options: It might be time to cash in a pension. I look into my box of 'valuables'. I wonder if my stash of old Cheltenham Town match-day programmes are worth anything. Yes – it's that bad. No stone will be left unturned. Nothing is safe. I find the 'Man on the Moon' first-day cover my father gave a rather impressionable young me in 1969. After forty years of meticulous care, now wasn't the time to discover it was the most widely distributed first-day cover **ever**.

A week later my face is pressed against the lounge window while I watch next-doors' cat on its regular patrol. While I'm determined to make the most of the time I have left, I can't be reckless. June has retired and I'm not going to leave her, or anybody else for that matter, with money worries. There isn't the money for a lavish world tour in any case. I've decided, if the news is bad, that 'Sandy Coloured Products' will have to continue their quest for world domination without me. I'm not currently in any pain so the present is as good as it will ever be and I have to make the most of it. Any funds I can rustle together will be used to finance an extremely modest lifestyle for the next two years until the cavalry (in the form of my state pension) come galloping over the horizon. I've no idea what kind of health issues I'll be confronted with by then.

Postscript

I lean there watching my breath condense on the window pane. I let it build up – I let it block the world out. My mind drifts away. I want to stop the world, but the lounge clock ticks relentlessly on.
Then there's a rattle from the letter box in the hall. I snap out of my trance and wipe the window pane in time to see the post-lady disappear down the drive. It's a familiar post-mark these days: my appointment letters. I used to rush headlong to the doormat in times gone by – but not so much now.
I have an appointment for an MRI scan in two weeks' time and a follow-up 'MRI result' appointment with my oncology specialist four weeks after that. I know it takes four weeks for the MRI scan results to become available, so this follow-up appointment would clearly be the one where I would learn my fate. Whether my world will be blown apart. Another letter details the first two appointments of my radiotherapy course, which consist of an introductory talk and a CT scan. I note that the radiotherapy appointments themselves are scheduled after my 'MRI result' appointment. This all makes sense given the circumstances. I conclude that if the news is bad he'll be able to pull the plug on my radiotherapy in favour of some more lavish course of treatment. Naturally I could just phone him up and get him to confirm, but there would be more chance of getting through to Elvis Presley.
I have six weeks to flutter about in a fool's paradise. If it's bad news, I need to make it palatable. I'm thinking of sweetening the pill by lavishing some money on an old sports car. This isn't as reckless as it sounds. It can simply be sold on without much depreciation once I'm unable to drive it.

I pray that nothing disturbs my course of radiotherapy. I don't tell family and friends that it's conditional on a satisfactory MRI scan,

Postscript

so I'm met with sympathetic glances and talk about survival rates when I tell them I'm in for radiotherapy. They don't realise I'd drop my trousers and be radiated there and then, given a chance.

I keep busy and try and banish those anxious thoughts. A specialist with a trained eye has spotted a problem in my pelvis. Most of the time I can forget about it, and I do -but my back is providing corroborating evidence. My back-ache has returned and I can't shift it - despite my carpet-hugging back exercises.

My daughter hasn't said she's worried about me in so many words but we've touched upon subjects that are outside the normal range. I do this calmly because my optimistic nature still prevails. We while away the hours in her garden in the wonderful Easter weather of 2019. It's good to talk –especially when someone's saying nice things. Only after an hour or so do I notice that my son-in-law has thoughtfully occupied the attentions of my granddaughter. It cannot last. I've got to give my granddaughter yet another 'horsey ride' and she won't wait any longer. Eventually it's time to go. I give my granddaughter a hug:
'Was I the bestest horse you ever rode?'
There's no reply, just a winning smile:
'Was I the bestest rider?'

Two weeks have come and gone and the MRI scan is something of an anti-climax -especially if you've had one before. I'm convinced the space-age sounds, the whirring and vibration is just a mechanism for justifying the price tag. Underneath the housing there's probably just a student with a sketch pad.
Four weeks now until my appointment with the Oncology specialist.

Of course, away from the hospital I have my moments. Sometimes I really need to talk, but this cancer lark is a lonely business. The occupational nurse is one of the very few people I've spoken to about my illness. When I go into detail the words come out of me in an unemotional way because they don't belong to me. I haven't adopted them yet. I'm just reciting them from someone else's script.

I'd love to unburden myself, but it's not fair on people. My words will put them in an awkward place. It would be comfort enough to know that someone is listening. I promise not to make myself a nuisance. I'll know when to stop and I won't over-indulge, but who do I talk to?

I'm sat in a large briefing room. Sandy Coloured Products want to update everyone on the merger. They also want to announce their 'Charity of Choice' for the next financial year. The announcement is made and a representative of the charity walks to the rostrum. She can't help but notice me —I'm sat bolt upright and suddenly I'm the most attentive person in the room. She explains the work of the 'Maggies' cancer support charity. They provide support to cancer sufferers and counselling is something they specialise in. I try not to see this as somehow prophetic.

My first radiotherapy appointment consists of an introductory talk with other patients. The nurse hosting the talk goes into fine detail about how to prepare for a radiotherapy session. The radiotherapy will be aimed with great precision at the target area with the help of some 'cross-hair' markers tattooed onto my hips.

I'm beginning to learn that nothing happens without some contributory pain and sacrifice from the patient. It seems to be part of the deal. For my part, I have to ensure that the area once

Postscript

occupied by my prostate (the 'bed' of the prostate) is in exactly the same place for every radiotherapy session. This requires that I hold about 400ml of urine in my bladder and that my rectum is empty. Getting the urine volume correct is just a combination of drinking and emptying, and will be checked using an ultrasound scan. Ensuring your rectum is completely empty is another matter.

Now if you've already decided to get yourself checked out, you can bail out at this point. I won't be disappointed in you. Early diagnosis will probably mean you'll be spared the next stage in any case.

Seriously, put the book down and find something more productive to do. The lawn looks like it needs mowing.

Ok. You're still here. Yes -the rectum is another matter. I will have to **ensure** this is empty by squirting the contents of a little tube up my own bottom. Thirty-three times.

With the results of my MRI scan still unknown, I realise that I still have to qualify for this privilege. Doing the daily squirt is far better than the alternative. It means I will only have been a temporary member if the Cancer Club.

It's not all bad. While I am still able, I'm doing a few adventures. I'm walking the Cornish coastal footpath. I keep going until dusk when I get my bivvy bag out and sleep under the stars. It's late-spring and the nights are getting warmer. June would normally frown on such silliness but I'm being indulged again -sleeping in the open matches my rather modest bucket-list budget.

It's the day of my 'MRI result' appointment. I haven't slept very well. I look around the waiting room. People are lost in their thoughts. I've been rehearsing my questions if things are bleak. I hope I can stay calm. This time I think I'm ready if the news is bad, but of course I'm kidding myself. I'll only hear the first couple of

Postscript

sentences and the rest of the consultant's transmission will be lost in interference as my mind loses the frequency.

I'm unknowing, almost naïvely uninformed. But not for much longer. Soon the consultant will hurry me across the rubicon into a whole new world. A world with closer horizons and a new way of looking at things. The old me will disappear, and there will be no point in trying to find him again. No point in looking back.

After an hour in the waiting room there's a voice. June looks at me –then stands up. I rise. All I see is the distant door. I'm through it into a corridor then it's the same scruffy depressing room we saw six weeks ago.

'Make yourself comfortable -he'll be along in a moment.'

The door is left open. I look out into the corridor. Staff hustle by at regular intervals. There's a rustle of clothes and a rhythmic squeak. A trolley goes past. My stomach churns. I'm trying to stay calm but my cheek suddenly develops a nervous tic. I hear voices outside. I'm trying to remember what my oncology specialist sounds like. Steps approach the door.

Suddenly he's appears in the office and the door is closed behind him.

'Good morning Mr Meredith'

I manage a tight smile. I throw a glance at June. He's scanning some paperwork.

'Hmmm….'

My eyes are fixed on the paperwork. A pause. He's tapping his pen now.

After what seemed like an age, he looks up. I can hardly meet his gaze. I don't want to engage with him. Suddenly his lips move –Oh God be kind.

'Your MRI scan is re-assuring'
More good words from the consultant but I've missed them. I'm trying to re-gain my composure.
I cling to the 're-assuring' word. It is, as you might expect, incredibly re-assuring.
He's now talking about the radiotherapy, so I've clearly jumped another hurdle. A vision of a squirty enema tube pops into my head. This would ordinarily provoke feelings of revulsion, but it's a testament to the circumstances I now find myself in that it's greeted almost with joy. Well almost.
He tells me that radiotherapy has a two-thirds success rate. Success being defined as zero PSA at the end of the treatment. A two-thirds success rate is a bit less than I was expecting. It becomes apparent that falling at this hurdle means your prostate cancer has already gone exploring. I'm leaving further questions for another day because I can't maintain concentration. So I've cleared a hurdle today but more are coming into view. This might be one race where jumping hurdles is infinitely preferable to crossing the finishing line. Those sunlit uplands I once dreamt of gambolling across are receding from view.

Back at Sandy Coloured Products, I inform HR (Human Resources) about my two-thirds radiotherapy success probability. I also float the idea of voluntary redundancy, given that my reduced working week means I can't respond so well to deadlines. I provide some good financial reasons why it might benefit both parties.

My proposal has prompted a meeting with HR. They have turned up in force and they start by discussing my radiotherapy appointments.

Postscript

It's clear from the amount of paperwork coming across the table towards me that HR have spent some time preparing for this meeting. This is of course quite humbling and reassuring. I still feel a fraud and it's all slightly surreal –like cancer is having a joke on me. I'm brimming with energy, actually feeling quite wonderful and take no medication for anything. Have the medical profession muddled me up with someone else? I'm told that if I'm unable to do my current job because of the side-effects of radiotherapy, I can cut my hours down further without loss of pay. I can even be given some alternative, less demanding job. The managing director's role comes into the discussion at this point – it's all good-humoured stuff and I express my gratitude at the company's response to my situation. I'm relieved that I can get on with my treatment without having to worry about my job situation and slightly embarrassed about the amount of attention I'm getting.

There's a pause.

Another HR lady enters the discussion for the first time. She also has a pile of paperwork in front of her and I sense it's coming my way. The tempo of the meeting changes gear and we head into uncharted territory –at least for me.

'We've taken note of the potential success rate for your radiotherapy and with this in mind we think we need to move the discussion into more delicate areas.'

She looked at her colleague.

'I'm afraid we won't consider redundancy while there's a chance that things might not turn out well for you. It wouldn't be in your best interests. I'll explain why.'

The potential gravity of my situation was coming home to me – despite my rude health. The full range of the company's death-in-service benefits were now revealed. Like I've found the secret

Postscript

doorway into Narnia. The probate service, counselling, free legal advice and my salary arrangements in the event I never return to work. Then there are the considerable benefits that will accrue to my dependents in the event that I never find my way back to the secret door. It's clear to me that in my current situation this is by far the best course of action for both myself and all those dear to me. I'm touched that they haven't accepted my ill-informed offer and used it as an opportunity to throw me on the scrap heap. I realise I am fortunate compared to some in my position.

'We just want you to have all the information you need. We had a case recently where someone passed away after a short illness and we almost didn't have time to have this discussion.'
I recalled a colleague who died suddenly.
She pushed a number of documents towards me:
'This is just precautionary. Chances are this will all be unnecessary and this will all end up in the bin.'
She looked at her colleague:
'We're here to support you all the way.'
My sense of relief was almost overwhelming. Only now do I realise how anxious I'd been about all this. I'm holding myself together now –as best I can.
'I..uh..I really appreciate this.'
Of course, the companys' intentions aren't purely altruistic, they have a legal duty to provide adequately for this situation. They know this – I know this, but it's incredibly re-assuring to feel the hooves of the HR cavalry under your feet as they charge over the hill to your rescue.
'Dave..'
The HR lady looked me in the eye:

'….we're going to work together on this. You focus on getting better. We'll look after the finances.'
I was lost for words. I'd carried the yoke of financial responsibility for a long long time. Her words lifted the burden from my shoulders.

There's something interesting in the post. Something quite exclusive. Something that reflects my stage in life. It's not a back-stage pass for Gardner's Question Time. It's a temporary parking permit for that most sought after of venues -the hospital car park. Never, even in my most delusional moments, did I think I could escape the clutches of the medical profession for ever, but neither could I imagine that my hospital visits would be so regular that I'd be allocated my own parking space. This has been issued in readiness for my thirty-three daily radiotherapy sessions. At least I will be spared the daily hassle of trying to find somewhere to park.

I'm half way through my radiotherapy sessions now. Of course, with my regular appointments and privileged parking space, I'm no longer the lost boy on his first day at school. I now exude confidence and bonhomie. I'm part of the hospital establishment. I even nod respectfully to members of staff. Every appointment starts with an ultrasound scan of my bladder. If it's too full I will decant into the nearest loo, if it's too low I will be sent away to drink a bit more. I engage the staff in a prediction competition. They rely on technology, I rely on discomfort. As the weeks go by I'm getting to know my bladder and my predictions are consistently within 50ml of the ultrasound reading. Not the kind of thing you'd boast about on 'Tinder' I suppose, but it lightens the mood.

Postscript

I'm approached on my latest visit by a dis-orientated elderly couple:
'Do you know the way to radiotherapy?'

I think back to when I was first married and money was in short supply. We were desperate for a carpet and I'd spotted a bargain off-cut on a foraging mission one work-day lunchtime. It could be ours if I could knock another fiver off. Unfortunately, an elderly couple were also showing an uncomfortable level of interest. They were already looking around for a member of staff. They were heading in my direction. My father had always insisted that in the ultra-competitive cut-throat world of work, the wearing of a shirt and tie would give me a competitive advantage. And so it proved on that particular day.
They made eye contact:
'I wonder if you can help us. We're interested in this carpet.'
I *needed* this carpet. I adjusted my tie and improvised:
'Ah well...'
I looked furtively around the shop.
'I shouldn't tell you this but there's a slight fault near the end of the roll'.
They were so grateful that I'd taken them into my confidence that they couldn't leave the store quick enough. I even got a little wave as they walked out the door.
I was astonished at my cheek but desperate times called for desperate measures.

Back to the present. My newly mature and philosophical self resists the temptation to send fellow sufferers elsewhere so I can have the treatment room all to myself.

Postscript

'Ah, Radiotherapy! Take the lift to the west wing, turn left at oncology and follow the corridor past the cafeteria. I'm going there myself'.
They follow. The corridors are pleasingly familiar these days and I aspire to be on first name terms with the receptionist.

At the end of my radiotherapy sessions my PSA will be measured again and another hurdle will be prepared. While I'm still feeling ok, I ensure that every day brims with possibility. Not always possible when the lawn wants mowing but you get the idea.

I've stopped jogging although my back is better. My reasoning is that this should lower my metabolism. I don't want to give my cancer fugitive a super-highway to go exploring on. I need to slow him, set some road blocks. That's my theory anyway – maybe I just feel that after thirty-five years of running, any accrued benefits are already in the bank. I've now finished my radiotherapy and have taken a PSA test. An appointment looms with the oncology specialist where I will find out if the radiotherapy has been a success. I now expect the worst and have my questions ready on a piece of paper. I'll try not to lose my composure this time. I'm better prepared. I already know where the Chemotherapy department is, should I need it. It's next to 'nuclear medicine' - whatever that is. I try and limit my curious nature – curiosity killed the cat.

Tomorrow, I'll attend my appointment with the oncology specialist clutching my pen and piece of paper. Over two years have now elapsed since the Urinary Tract Infection that started my cancer journey. I'm going to leave you unsure of the outcome. That's because I want you to experience the sheer uncertainty of life after

Postscript

a cancer diagnosis. It's beyond the scope of this book to describe what it's like to be a permanent member of the Cancer Club. Despite my thoroughness, all I'm really doing **as I write these words** is checking out the facilities. My aim with this postscript is to encourage you to get yourself checked out. I can't help but notice how kind people are once they know I am ill. They would be kind to you given the chance. Are you going to give them the opportunity? Do you really want a ride on the cancer roller coaster? Early diagnosis is essential for good outcomes, so get yourself checked out –today.

Appendix 1

My Treatment Timeline
Only principal appointments are shown.

2017

July Doctor visit for UTI. PSA test

September 5th Appointment for discussion of PSA results and DRE.

November 11th Biopsy and fitting of catheter.

2018

January 2nd **2018** Biopsy result (cancer).

January 24th Bone scan.

January 29th Bone scan results.

February 6th Outpatient appointment with surgeon.

February 12th. Switch to self-catheterising.

March 14th Pre-operation assessment and consent form.

March 28th Prostatectomy Operation

April 10th 2018 Catheter removal, stitch removal and trial voiding.

2019

June-Aug Radiotherapy

Appendix 2
Lessons Learnt

Don't underestimate the healing power of kind words, gestures and 'get well' cards.

Try and find out as much as you can about your family's medical history.

Proper rest is the quickest route to recovery.

Keep yourself busy during those long weeks of waiting

During the time you have your catheter drink loads. Then drink some more.

If you're having a catheter removed -don't be frightened to ask the nurse to take it slowly.

After you've emptied your leg bag, don't forget to close the drain tap. Forgetting to close the tap on your bed-bag doesn't even bear thinking about.

By all means get comfortable and confident with the in-dwelling catheter. Whatever you do don't get careless. Always check the drain tap isn't visible!

Always take someone with you when you attend your consultant appointments. Not so important for a routine blood test, but when bad news is flowing past your ears, you'll need someone else to catch the words and take them home for you.

Feeling low? Help a person in need, or just do a favour for someone. It might take your mind off your own troubles. It worked for me. God knows why.

Be as public or as private as you want to be, but bear in mind you will need areas of your life (your workplace for example) where you can be free to forget about cancer for a while.

Appendix 3
My medical 'Bucket List'

I have been fortunate to have enjoyed reasonably good health all my life so many of the procedures I underwent during my illness were being experienced for the first time.

Ultrasound Scan
MRI Scan
Bone Scan
In-dwelling catheter
Single-use catheter
Stitch removal
Drain tube removal
DRE (Digital Rectal Examination)
Biopsy
Enema
Self-injecting

Appendix 4
My prostate -do I need it?

The prostate plays a number of roles in your urinary and reproductive systems. The urethra passes through the prostate, and there is a sphincter muscle at the base of the prostate which helps you remain continent. The loss of this means that continence has to be regained by other means.

The nerves which control your erections surround it the prostate. It's not the loss of the prostate itself that causes erectile dysfunction, but damage to the nerves themselves.

The prostate is largely responsible for the physical aspects of the ejaculation itself, and the semen it contains. The prostate secretes fluid that nourishes and protects sperm. The milky fluid produced by the prostate – prostatic fluid – makes up around 30 percent of the total fluid ejaculated (the rest is sperm and fluid from the seminal vesicles). Prostatic fluid protects sperm, helping them live longer and be more mobile. During ejaculation, the prostate squeezes prostatic fluid into the urethra, and it is expelled with sperm as part of semen.

So that little organ that you hardly knew anything about is pretty important. This is why incontinence and erectile dysfunction are side effects of prostatectomy. Every operation is to a certain extent unique in terms of the damage done to the nerves surrounding the prostate. This is why every recovery is different regarding erectile dysfunction and continence.

Postscript

Printed in Great Britain
by Amazon